Richard Maidstone

Concordia
(The Reconciliation of Richard II with London)

Middle English Texts

General Editor

Russell A. Peck
University of Rochester

Associate Editor

Alan Lupack
University of Rochester

Assistant Editor

Dana M. Symons
University of Rochester

Advisory Board

Rita Copeland
University of Pennsylvania

Thomas G. Hahn
University of Rochester

Lisa Kiser
Ohio State University

R. A. Shoaf
University of Florida

Bonnie Wheeler
Southern Methodist University

The Middle English Texts Series is designed for classroom use. Its goal is to make available to teachers and students texts that occupy an important place in the literary and cultural canon but have not been readily available in student editions. The series does not include those authors, such as Chaucer, Langland, or Malory, whose English works are normally in print in good student editions. The focus is, instead, upon Middle English literature adjacent to those authors that teachers need in compiling the syllabuses they wish to teach. The editions maintain the linguistic integrity of the original work but within the parameters of modern reading conventions. Middle English Texts Series includes a few adjunct texts that are in a language other than English. These texts are intimately tied to Middle English writers, their English writings, or the political and social scene in which they write. These volumes differ from the TEAMS Documents of Practice Series in that the focus is always to be literary. Sometimes the texts will be by writers who are well known for their work in English. The foreign language texts are printed with facing-page translations and include explanatory as well as textual notes. The adjunct volumes will occasionally include appendices to assist in identifying the centrality of the work to literary activities.

Richard Maidstone

Concordia
(The Reconciliation of
Richard II with London)

with a verse translation by
A. G. Rigg

Edited by
David R. Carlson

Published for TEAMS
(The Consortium for the Teaching of the Middle Ages)
in Association with the University of Rochester

by

MEDIEVAL INSTITUTE PUBLICATIONS
College of Arts and Sciences
Western Michigan University
Kalamazoo, Michigan
2003

Library of Congress Cataloging-in-Publication Data

Maidstone, Richard, d. 1396.
  [Concordia facta inter regem et cives Londonie. English & Latin]
  Concordia : the reconciliation of Richard II with London / with a
verse translation by A.G. Rigg ; edited by David R. Carlson.
       p. cm. -- (Middle English texts)
Includes bibliographical references.
  ISBN 1-58044-080-0 (pbk. : alk. paper)
  1. Richard II, King of England, 1367-1400--Poetry. 2. London
(England)--History--To 1500--Poetry. I. Title: Reconciliation of
Richard II with London. II. Rigg, A. G. III. Carlson, David R. (David
Richard), 1956- IV. Consortium for the Teaching of the Middle Ages. V.
Title. VI. Middle English texts (Kalamazoo, Mich.)
  PA8547.M26C66 2003
  821'.1--dc22
                                                  2003018279

ISBN 1-58044-080-0

Printed in the United States of America

Cover design by Linda K. Judy

Contents

Acknowledgments

Russell A. Peck made arrangements for the volume to be included as an adjunct volume to the Middle English Texts Series and gave the manuscript an initial reading and critique. Michael Livingston gave the volume its initial format; he suggested various corrections, helped to match punctuation between the Latin text and English translation, entered corrections, and prepared final camera-ready copy. Emily Rebekah Huber gave the introduction a preliminary reading with an eye toward stylistic revision. Annie Heckel proofread and adjusted the appendices to the style of the series, did additional formatting, and entered corrections. John Chandler also read the manuscript at a late stage. As Assistant Editor of the Middle English Texts Series, Dana M. Symons gave the manuscript its initial and final proofreadings. At Medieval Institute Publications, Patricia Hollahan and her staff gave the manuscript one last assessment and registered the volume with the Library of Congress. We are grateful to the National Endowment for the Humanities for their generous support throughout the project.

Concordia facta inter regem et cives Londonie

Introduction

1. The Metropolitan Crisis of 1392

The London troubles of 1392 were not as spectacular as the armed clashes between England's king and magnates of adjacent years. In those, people died: in the Battle of Radcot Bridge during the Appellants' coup in December, 1387; in King Richard's bloody reprisals of 1397; or, ultimately, in Henry of Lancaster's armed invasion of 1399 that culminated in Richard's deposition and murder. About the magnate opposition to Richard II, there was much nostalgia, as if the fundamental issues of disposable power in the kingdom might be resolved by applications of noble muscularity, through exercise of the heroism of a chivalric or epic golden age.[1] The conflict between the city of London — more specifically, the merchant-oligarchs there commanding a particular kind of fiscal power deriving from their city-based activities — and King Richard II that came to a crisis point in 1392 was quieter, inasmuch as the kind of power at issue was more abstract, more modern, so to speak. The conflict was financial. King Richard needed money. The corporation of the city of London and various eminent citizens were believed to have it. When, for a variety of reasons, the civic merchants hesitated to avail, the king made them give. By a series of extraordinary measures, the city was forced to submit, paying the king off lavishly and acknowledging its submission by public ceremonial on 21–22 August 1392. It was in response to these events that Richard Maidstone wrote the Latin poem, *Concordia facta inter regem et cives Londonie.*[2]

---

[1] Mervyn James, "English Politics and the Concept of Honour, 1485–1642."

[2] The poem has been edited twice before, one of these previous editions having been published twice, the other not at all: by Thomas Wright, in *Alliterative Poem on the Deposition of Richard II*, pp. 31–51, an edition reprinted, evidently without recourse to the original manuscript, in *Political Poems and Songs Relating to English History Composed during the Period from the Accession of EDW. III. to That of RIC. III.* 1.282–300; and then by Charles Roger Smith, in an unpublished doctoral thesis, "*Concordia: Facta inter Regem Riccardum II et civitatem Londonie per Fratrum Riccardum Maydiston, Carmelitam, Sacre Theologie Doctorem, Anno Domine 1393*, edited with Introduction, Translation, and Notes." Smith's translation is often fanciful and occasionally wrong. A good portion of the poem is translated, too, in Glynne Wickham, *Early English Stages 1300 to 1660* 1.64–71, quoting from Wright's 1859 edition.

For what follows, on the background to the 1392 crisis, see especially Ruth Bird, *The Turbulent London*

Concordia facta inter regem et cives Londonie

The city had been manifestly troubled throughout the reign of Richard II. On the one hand, conflicts between class factions within the city — above all between the merchant capitalists, concentrated amongst the vintners, fishmongers, grocers, mercers, and goldsmiths, whose wealth derived from distribution and exchange, and the artisans and small masters of the city, whose wealth was based on production and consumption — became acute during this period, by consequence of the growth of trade-based wealth and finance in the city, at the expense of production.[3] An effort at city-constitutional reform, codified by the "Good Parliament" of 1376, to redress the balance of power in favor of the more productive but less concentratedly wealthy elements in the city — including even an experiment akin to soviet-style election of city officials by guild membership in place of ward residence — led eventually to street fighting and armed insurrection when the militant populist leader of the reformers amongst the smaller productive elements, John Northampton, failed to win reelection to a third term as mayor in October, 1383. Northampton was condemned and temporarily banished from the city, and he never after had a part in city affairs; the crisis brought by the constitutional reform movement strengthened the oligarchy's hold on power in the city to such a degree that, even after Northampton's antagonist Nicholas Brembre — the wealthiest of the merchant oligarchs by a considerable margin — was executed in 1388 for his adherence to Richard II, the oligarchic faction was still not dislodged from internal city politics. To the contrary, "Brembre's ruin was personal: the power of the capitalist party in London remained unshaken," as Ruth Bird has said; the reform effort and its sequels in the end yielded a strengthened oligarchy:

> The constitutional history of the City of London during the twenty years 1376–97 is the history of an attempt so to change the forms of the constitution that the monopoly of political power held by a small number of wealthy men might be broken. These changes in form, though successfully carried out, failed to effect the desired result; but they had given rise to such opportunities of friction and violence, between classes and between misteries, that the victorious capitalist party reversed them — actuated probably also by the fear that they might be of effective use in the future — and substituted a system in some ways even more favourable to an oligarchy than that which had existed before the conflict began.[4]

---

of Richard II, and the important revisionary paper of Pamela Nightingale, "Capitalists, Crafts and Constitutional Change in Late Fourteenth-Century London"; for the events of 1392, I rely chiefly on Caroline M. Barron, "The Quarrel of Richard II with London 1392-7."

[3] Nightingale, "The Growth of London in the Medieval English Economy," especially pp. 99–101. The development is treated in greater detail in Gwyn A. Williams, *Medieval London: From Commune to Capital*, chs. 5 ("The Mercantile Interests") and 6 ("The Rise of the Crafts"), pp. 106–95.

[4] Bird, *Turbulent London*, pp. 99, 30.

On the other hand, there were in the same period conflicts between the corporate body of the city of London and the English landed aristocracy, the monarch in particular. In pursuit of various objectives in areas ranging from temporary personal advantage to international diplomacy, various aristocrats, the king leading, were inclined to interfere in city politics. The mayor Brembre's eventually fatal adherence to the king, like the transient support that Northampton enjoyed from John of Gaunt, suggests already that city-internal matters might become implicated in national and international affairs. "The really disruptive force in the community of London," Pamela Nightingale has said, "was the crown."[5] Its disruptions were concentrated chiefly in two areas: the franchise of the city, by which participation in retail redistribution of goods was restricted to freemen of the city, thereby excluding not only foreign merchants, but also provincial immigrants and the unenfranchised (i.e., about two-thirds of the population of the city); and the staple system, by which the export of English goods, chiefly wool, was regulated, with consequences also for imports and their distribution, to the benefit or injury of the London merchant-capitalists.[6] In the long term, maintenance of the staple system was in the interest of the monarchy too, inasmuch as the taxes it might impose on the trade passing through the port of London and the overseas staples could provide the crown with reliable income; its regular taxation of imports and exports also provided the crown with security for loans it might require, which it could and generally did repay by farming out collection of some portion of a tax to its creditors.[7] But in response to various short-term exigencies — most often a need to raise money immediately, though also in reaction to continental affairs and diplomatic objectives — the crown chose from time to time to abrogate or to alter the staple system, or to manipulate the franchise. For example, in 1378 the crown decided to raise money for itself by selling Genoese merchants licenses to import and export goods through the port of Southampton rather than London, thereby bypassing the staples. The ramifications of this decision have recently been explored by Paul Strohm.[8] The situation was additionally complicated by the participation of non-civic landed interests in financial affairs too, extending or withholding loans to the crown, for example, as well as in trade (the wool trade especially), sometimes in competition with the more extensively capitalized London merchant-oligarchs.[9]

---

[5] Nightingale, "Capitalists, Crafts and Constitutional Change," p. 34. A succinct delineation of the lines of force, likewise emphasizing the role of the crown, is in George Unwin, *The Gilds and Companies of London*, especially pp. 127–33.

[6] Nightingale, "Capitalists, Crafts and Constitutional Change," especially pp. 8–16.

[7] See Eileen Power, *The Wool Trade in English Medieval History*, especially pp. 86–103, on the staple system.

[8] Paul Strohm, "Trade, Treason, and the Murder of Janus Imperial."

[9] In general, see Nightingale, "Knights and Merchants: Trade, Politics and the Gentry in Late Medieval England"; the specific case of the involvement in trade and finance of the Fitzalan earls of Arundel, who,

Concordia facta inter regem et cives Londonie

In 1391, as on various earlier occasions, the crown banned denizen wool exports and suspended the foreign staples, removing such trade from the control of the London merchant-oligarchs, encouraging foreign merchants, and also giving incentive for use of other English ports, like Southampton or Hull, in place of London.[10] Loans from city merchants to the crown had already dried up by this point in any event: the last corporate loan from the city to the crown had come in 1388, and loans from individual franchise-holders of the city also came to a stop, falling from over £1,500 in 1388, to about £500 in 1389, to just more than £200 in 1390, and then to none at all in 1391.[11] The immediate occasion for letting slip the royal wrath (according to some of the contemporary chronicle accounts) may have been provided by an armed city mob attacking the London palace of the caesarean bishop of Salisbury John Waltham, also royal treasurer and lord keeper of the privy seal, the culmination of what might otherwise have been a minor dispute over non-payment of a retail trade-bill. With the support of the archbishop of York Thomas Arundel, also lord chancellor, Waltham petitioned the king for redress of the Londoners' commercial extortions. There was also complaint of the Londoners' propensity for harboring heretical religions.[12]

In May 1392, King Richard informed the city of his intention to remove the court of common pleas to York on account of the truculence of London, and a general administrative removal took place. For the duration of 1392, in addition to the common bench, the rolls of the king's bench, the Fleet prison, the exchequers of accounts, of pleas, and of receipt, and the chancery were removed from the metropolis.[13] At the end of the same May, Richard summoned the elected mayor, sheriffs, and aldermen of the city to appear before king and royal council at Nottingham. At the Nottingham session, 25 June, king and council deposed the elected mayor and the sheriffs and imprisoned them, replacing them with a royally chosen warden of the city and royally chosen sheriffs, who were installed in London by 29 June. On 27 June, the king empowered a royal commission "to enquire into the notorious defaults in the government of the city of London."[14] About fifty of the civic governors of the city — present and past mayors, sheriffs, and aldermen — were summoned to appear before the commission.

---

for example, substantially financed Edward III's military adventures but withheld all credit from Richard II, is analyzed in Chris Given-Wilson, "Wealth and Credit, Public and Private: The Earls of Arundel 1306–1397."

[10] Nightingale, "Capitalists, Crafts and Constitutional Change," p. 32.

[11] Barron, "The Quarrel of Richard II," p. 178n16.

[12] Bird, *Turbulent London*, pp. 106–08; Barron, "The Quarrel of Richard II," pp. 180–81.

[13] T. F. Tout, *Chapters in the Administrative History of Mediaeval England*, 6 vols. (Manchester: Manchester University Press, 1920–33; rpt. 1967), 3.481–82. Such offices returned to London only in early 1393.

[14] Barron, "The Quarrel of Richard II," p. 185.

On 22 July, at Eton, the commission convicted them "by their own acknowledgment," fined them 3,000 marks, and pronounced the liberties of the city forfeited to the king.[15] Additionally, the king laid a corporate fine of £100,000 on the city and took steps to bring immediately into his disposal the city's entire income, "mortgaged to pay this enormous sum."[16]

Caroline Barron has described these royal actions as considerate extortion, "devised over a period of months, if not years," and sprung on the city "by surprise attack."[17] The city could only capitulate. The negotiations of the terms of the capitulation, by which the king was eventually reconciled to the city, are not on record, but that a reconciliation had been effected was made public by the king's pageantic reentry into the city, 21 August 1392. A series of subsequent royal acts gave substance to the reconciliation: on 17 September, the city was enjoined to elect its own sheriffs; on 19 September, by a series of royal pardons issued from Woodstock, the fines and terms of imprisonment imposed on the deposed and former mayors, sheriffs, and aldermen were pardoned, the corporate fine of £100,000 was forgiven, and the liberties of the city were restored, albeit only "until the king shall otherwise ordain."[18] In October, the city elected its own mayor to replace the still serving royal warden, and the common bench and other administrative offices of state were bidden to return from the north.

This settlement's cost to the city is put in the chronicles at £20,000 to £40,000 cash paid to the king, though the royal receipt of 28 February 1393 was for only £10,000. The cash was raised within the city from various sources and by various means, evidently on a broad basis: "there was a civic tax collected in the wards assessed on lands and rents," for example; the widows and clergy of London complained to parliament of the imposition, and, according to one chronicler, numerous citizens fled the city in order to avoid compulsory contribution.[19] In addition to financing the pageant entry of August, the city also paid some of the costs of the king's Christmas-time entertainment at Eltham for 1392–93 and sent lavish gifts; "in the following summer of 1393, at Richard's express command, the wardens of London Bridge paid Thomas Wreuk, a mason, to carve two stone statues of the king and queen to be placed above the stone gate on the bridge"; and in December 1394 the city loaned Richard a further 10,000 marks, which the king did eventually repay.[20] Still, the city's liberties were not properly

---

[15] Barron, "The Quarrel of Richard II," p. 187. According to the *OED* (*mark*, sb.2, 2a), "after the Conquest . . . the value of the mark became fixed at 160 pence . . . or 2/3 of the £ sterling." Thus, the fine on the governors amounted to £2,000.

[16] Barron, "The Quarrel of Richard II," p. 189.

[17] Barron, "The Quarrel of Richard II," p. 181.

[18] Barron, "The Quarrel of Richard II," p. 191.

[19] Barron, "The Quarrel of Richard II," p. 195.

[20] Barron, "The Quarrel of Richard II," pp. 195–96.

restored as a matter of right rather than royal pleasure until 1397, evidently at the cost of a "loan" of another 10,000 marks, which was not repaid.[21]

Not to mention the incalculable costs of lost and irreplaceable custom, in Barron's concluding estimate, "the citizens' aloof refusals in the years 1388–92, cost them in the succeeding five years £16,666 13s 4d in straight exactions, £10,000 or so in jewels and gifts, the costs of a magnificent reception and Christmas entertainment, and the new statuary on London Bridge; in all, perhaps, a total of £30,000. Clearly the poorer citizens, such as the widows and clergy who petitioned parliament in 1394, found these exactions hard to pay."[22] Other citizens would have felt differently, however, for a by-product of these royal extortions, even in the short term, was a redistribution of wealth within the city, incidental though not inconsiderable, from the poorer elements to the merchant-oligarchic few who enjoyed royal favor. Richard used the money he had extorted for a spending spree in the city:

> The wardrobe account for the years 1392–4 reveals that the king purchased over £13,000-worth of saddlery, mercery, skins and drapery in these two years. Only when the wardrobe was equipping Richard's two expeditions to Ireland did its expenditure exceed this amount. Of this £13,000 about 90 per cent went into the pockets of London merchant suppliers of whom the two most prominent were the draper, John Hende, the imprisoned mayor of 1392, and the young and rising mercer, Richard Whittington [whom Richard was to appoint mayor in extraordinary circumstances in 1397]. It may be, therefore, that much of the money which Richard extorted from the citizens found its way back into their pockets in the form of purchases for the royal wardrobe and household. Of course, far more Londoners contributed to the £10,000 fine [paid the king in early 1393] than acted as royal suppliers.[23]

In such a context, it may be difficult to see the point of the lavish pageantic entry that was staged for the king. By August, it would have been clear that the money was coming to him as fast as the city could gather it, and it might have been thought sufficient had he restored civic self-governance and quietly returned his administration to London. There is no evidence that the public ceremonial was a stipulated part of the deal by which the crisis was resolved, nor that the entry was requested by the king or suggested by his party, or whether it was simply a *douceur*, however excessive, offered spontaneously by the city.[24] In any case, the king is felt to have had

---

[21] Barron, "The Quarrel of Richard II," pp. 198–99.

[22] Barron, "The Quarrel of Richard II," p. 200.

[23] Barron, "The Quarrel of Richard II," p. 197.

[24] The phrase of the monk of Westminster ("ad hec clemens et benignus rex pietate motus ad instanciam domine regine aliorumque suorum procerum et magnatum remisit eis omnia que in eum deliquerunt sub ista condicione, quod infra decem annos proximo sequentes solvant ei aut ejus certis attornatis quadraginta milia librarum, et hoc ad verum valorem, videlicet in jocalibus aut in pecunia numerata, et quod venirent erga eum et exciperent eum aput Wandlesworthe decenti apparatu," etc.) may be taken to indicate that the

a fondness for this sort of thing, and the city was put to great trouble and expense about staging the entry; usually, though, with such Ricardian spectacles, something greater was in view than an infantile fascination with fripperies. For example, the point of the 1390 Smithfield tournament, which included a scripted pageantry in which Chaucer may have had a hand, was international and diplomatic. Sheila Lindenbaum has asserted that there was something financial in it for the merchantry of the city, too, in the form of monies brought into the city economy with the influx of rich visitors, the construction, the provisioning, and so forth.[25] But above all, Richard was keeping up with his French royal compeers. The entry into Paris of the Valois queen Isabella just months earlier was the avowed model. The tournament attracted various foreign participants, who would have returned to their homes with concrete evidence of the magnificence (and hence the disposable power) of the English monarch, however embattled he was in real albeit less public terms at the time. One of the featured foreign participants was a Count William of Ostrevant, with whom Richard needed an alliance, as Nigel Saul has pointed out, to further his anti-Valois continental agenda.[26] In addition to marking publicly the return of royal favor to the metropolis, the 1392 pageantry had also the larger purpose of articulating the conception of royal power animating Richard's actions at the time. Better than any other source, Maidstone's poem on the entry clarifies this larger political agenda. In a way done comparably only by such other contemporary documents as the chancellors' sermons with which the Ricardian parliaments were opened,[27] Maidstone's poem tells what Richard's objectives for his kingship were.

---

entry was a part of the settlement stipulated by King Richard; see below, Appendix 1.2.

[25] Sheila Lindenbaum, "The Smithfield Tournament of 1390." The commercial impact of provisioning such spectacle on the economy of the city of London, in the context of later occasions, is emphasized by Jennifer Loach, "The Function of Ceremonial in the Reign of Henry VIII," especially pp. 66–68.

[26] Nigel Saul, *Richard II*, pp. 351–52.

[27] Some information on such sermons is to be found in S. B. Chrimes, *English Constitutional Ideas in the Fifteenth Century*, pp. 142–45 and 165–91. Most pertinent here would be the chancellor's sermon that opened the "Revenge Parliament" in 1397, report of which is in John Strachey, ed., *Rotuli parliamentorum* 3.347: the chancellor, Edmund Stafford, bishop of Exeter (an Aegedian civil lawyer by training, and Richard's keeper of the privy seal, 1389–95), took as his text Ezekiel 37:22 ("Rex unus erit omnibus" ["There shall be one king over them all"]): "Allegeant sur ce [i.e., this text] pluseurs auctoritees de seinte escripture, que un roy et un governour serra, et que par autre manere nulle roialme purra estre governez, et que a la bone governance de chescun roy trois choses sont requis: primerement, que le roy soit puissant a governer; secondement, que les loies par queux il doit governer soient gardez et executz justement; tiercement, que les subgitz du roialme soient obeissantz duement a roy et ses loies" ["On the matter of this text adducing numerous authorities from holy writ, to the effect that a king and governor need be one and singular, for no realm can be governed otherwise; and that for purposes of any king's good governance three things are requisite: first, that the king should be possessed of the power necessary to govern; second, that the laws by means of which he needs govern should be justly respected

2. Richard Maidstone

The author of the poem *Concordia*, occasioned by this 1392 crisis, was Richard Maidstone, a Carmelite friar. A date for his birth in the 1350s, or possibly slightly earlier, may be inferred from his having entered his order by 1376 at the Aylesford Convent, Kent, the house where the order had been founded in England in 1242. There is record of Maidstone's ordination to the priesthood, by the bishop of Winchester William Wykeham, on 20 December 1376. After his death on 1 June 1396, he was buried in the cloister of the same Aylesford Convent. Meanwhile, Maidstone was licensed to preach and to hear confessions in the Rochester diocese, 24 March 1390, and, by the evidence of his own statements, he earned the B.D. and D.D. degrees at Oxford, though no records of the dates or other circumstances of the degrees' grantings have come to light.[28]

Maidstone was evidently a confessor to John of Gaunt, the over-mighty royal uncle, who had a history of meddling in London politics.[29] The anti-civic part he had to play in the "Good Parliament" in 1376 (both Edward III and the Black Prince were incapable at the moment) and Gaunt's public advocacy afterwards, during 1377, of proposals to abrogate salient civic liberties (including a proposal for royal appointment of a "captain" for London, to replace the traditional annual mayoral election) left residual resentment. Gaunt's city residence, the Savoy, attracted special attention in 1381 from the revolutionaries, who razed it — the only city property treated this way — pointedly not looting it beforehand.[30] In the same period, Gaunt lent equivocal, then diminishing support to the militant populist political reformer and mayor,

---

and enforced; and third, that subjects of the realm should be utterly submissive in their obedience to the king and his laws"]. Except where other translators are expressly credited (and aside from A. G. Rigg's verse translation of Maidstone's poem itself), all translations are the editor's.

[28] For particulars, see Alfred Brotherston Emden, *A Biographical Register of the University of Oxford to A. D. 1500* 2.1204.

[29] The only evidence is the statement in the heading of the *Protectorium pauperis* in the unique manuscript, Oxford, Bodleian Library, *e Mus*. 86, calling it the work "Ricardi Maydeston . . . illustrisimi principis domini Joannis ducis Lancastriae confessoris." See Valerie Edden, "The Debate between Richard Maidstone and the Lollard Ashwardby (ca. 1390)," p. 115n10. Bale had access to this manuscript, evidently, so his witness does not constitute independent confirmation.

[30] For Gaunt's interventions of 1376–77, see George Holmes, *The Good Parliament*, especially pp. 189–93, or Anthony Goodman, *John of Gaunt: The Exercise of Princely Power in Fourteenth-Century Europe*, pp. 55–62; and on events of 1381, see Steven Justice, *Writing and Rebellion: England in 1381*, pp. 23–24 and 90–101.

John Northampton, whom Thomas Usk the Chaucerian notoriously betrayed in 1383–84, after Northampton's defeat in the violently contested mayoral election of October, 1383.[31]

Gaunt is known to have favored the English Carmelites, and, by special papal dispensation, he did employ a series of distinguished Carmelites as personal confessors, including William Badby, Walter Diss, and John Kynyngham.[32] Gaunt is also known to have patronized writers, though the extent of his patronage and the policy or policies that might have animated it remain to be clarified by systematic study. Speght's 1602 assertion that Chaucer's "An ABC" was written at the request of Blanche, Gaunt's duchess, a similar though earlier assertion that the *Complaint of Mars* was written for Gaunt himself, the *Book of the Duchess* and the annuity Gaunt paid Chaucer from 1374 have suggested patronal favor for Chaucer as a writer, though the evidence is equivocal.[33] More certainly, Gaunt aided John Wyclif, though only early in Wyclif's controversial career, before the Blackfriars condemnation of 1382, by which point Gaunt's Carmelites had turned him against the heresiarch.[34] Moreover, Gaunt received the dedication of the *Kalendarium* of Nicholas of Lynn — another Carmelite — in 1386, having encouraged the work.[35] The nearest analogue possibly for Maidstone's *Concordia* may be the grand poem of Walter of Peterborough (who may also have been a confessor of Gaunt), written in about five hundred Latin elegiacs in celebration of the English victory at Najera in 1367. Walter praises Gaunt particularly, using the same sort of classicizing rhetoric that Maidstone was later to use in the *Concordia*. A verse preface surviving with one of the copies of Walter's effusion addresses the poem to Gaunt through the agency of the treasurer of Gaunt's

---

[31] Bird, *Turbulent London*, pp. 23–27 and 81–85.

[32] Goodman, *John of Gaunt*, pp. 244–48.

[33] The evidence on the circumstances of "An ABC" and the *Complaint of Mars* is reproduced in Eleanor Prescott Hammond, *Chaucer: A Bibliographical Manual*, pp. 355 and 384; on the *Book of the Duchess*, see Edward I. Condren, "The Historical Context of the *Book of the Duchess*: A New Hypothesis," and J[ohn] J. N. Palmer, "The Historical Context of the *Book of the Duchess*: A Revision"; and on the annuity and relations between Chaucer and Gaunt generally, see Derek Pearsall, *The Life of Geoffrey Chaucer: A Critical Biography*, pp. 82–84. The annual commemorative rite for Blanche (for one of which Chaucer's *Book of the Duchess* may have been written) described in N. B. Lewis, "The Anniversary Service for Blanche, Duchess of Lancaster, 12th September 1374," was administered by Carmelites.

[34] That Gaunt's support for Wyclif was persistent throughout Wyclif's career is the argument of Joseph H. Dahmus, *The Prosecution of John Wyclyf*, rehearsing the evidence for Gaunt's early support, especially pp. 7–19.

[35] In his preface, Nicholas asserts that he wrote "ad peticionem et complacenciam" of Gaunt; see Sigmund Eisner, ed., *The Kalendarium of Nicholas of Lynn*, p. 59. Nicholas's relations with Gaunt are discussed by Eisner, p. 2; see also the highly suggestive brief remarks of J. A. W. Bennett, *Chaucer at Oxford and at Cambridge*, pp. 76–77.

household, John Marton; but Walter was disappointed, it seems, for the same copy also includes a verse envoy in which the poet complains that the patronal munificence he had hoped to attract had not been forthcoming.[36]

Gaunt's personal interest in the 1392 metropolitan crisis would seem to have been limited. The monk of Westminster and Thomas Walsingham both name Gaunt among those who interceded on the city's behalf with the king, and, in October 1392, Gaunt and the other two royal uncles, Clarence and Gloucester, were given gifts of £400 and a gilt basin by a city delegation for reasons unspecified.[37] On the other hand, Gaunt was abroad, negotiating peace with the French, from mid-March until mid-May 1392, during a critical period, though he was present at various royal councils both before and afterwards. Most significantly, Gaunt was not appointed to the royal commission of inquiry — the one that summoned the Londoners to Eton, deposed the city government, and imposed the £100,000 fine, on 25–27 June 1392 — though the other royal uncles were. In mid-August, at the time of the pageantic reconciliation with the city, Gaunt was on some kind of holiday, hunting in the north of England.

Be this various evidence as it may, the fact remains that Maidstone does not mention Gaunt in the *Concordia* (nor in any of the other writings of his that have been published). The evidence that Maidstone was a confessor of Gaunt's seems reliable enough. Nevertheless, tantalizing as the inference may be, it cannot be corroborated that, in 1392 or on some other occasion, Maidstone may also have been in Gaunt's employ as a poet or may have enjoyed Gaunt's patronage for his literary efforts.

Even the most literary of Maidstone's surviving writings, an English paraphrase of the seven penitential psalms in some eight hundred lines of rhyming stanzaic verse,[38] suggests that he was an ideologue. "Avowedly orthodox, pro-ecclesiastical, pro-sacerdotal," the paraphrase is above all a *stimulus penitentiae* (the recurrent, quasi-refrain-like phrase it uses is a reminder that Christ "dere us bougte"), by which the reader is prepared to enter the more thoroughly into the sacrament of penance, confession particularly, requiring of course the church's mediation

---

[36] The poem is edited in Wright, *Political Poems and Songs* 1.97–122; on Walter and his writing, see A. G. Rigg, *A History of Anglo-Latin Literature, 1066–1422*, pp. 276–78. Palmer, "Froissart et le Héraut Chandos," especially pp. 276–81, shows reason to regard the Chandos Herald's life of the Black Prince as "un traité politique, assez subtil, écrit dans l'intérêt de Lancastre et déguisé en biographie" (p. 281).

[37] For these particulars, I rely on Goodman, *John of Gaunt*, pp. 149–52; see also Barron, "The Quarrel of Richard II," p. 194, on the city's gifts to the royal uncles. Evidently, the paying of such bribes to aristocrats was not otherwise unknown in this period; other examples are mentioned in Bird, *Turbulent London*, pp. 48–49.

[38] This work has been most recently edited by Valerie Edden, *Richard Maidstone's Penitential Psalms*; it was also published in Mabel Day, ed., *The Wheatley Manuscript*, pp. 19–59.

and the ministrations of a priest-confessor.[39] The Fourth Lateran Council's imposition of universally obligatory annual confession in 1215 had made this sacrament the central churchly intervention in the lives of lay persons, second only to the sacrifice of the Mass; moreover, by contrast with the Mass, to the degree that confession was personal and involved more active lay participation, it was the more effective institutional tool for indoctrination, akin to preaching in this respect, only more coercive inasmuch as the priest-confessor was endowed with effective power to withhold absolution. As Eamon Duffy delicately asserts, "in principle, this ruling [of the Fourth Lateran] put into the hands of the parish clergy an immensely valuable pastoral and educational tool, for the priest in confession could explore not only the moral condition of his parishioners, but also their knowledge of Catholic faith and practice. . . . Confessional practice and the catechetical and preaching programme of the English Church in the fifteenth century were closely linked."[40]

By means of a series of local ecclesiastical constitutions — most influentially perhaps the Lambeth Constitutions of Pecham, archbishop of Canterbury, in 1281 and the Constitutions of Thoresby, archbishop of York, in 1357 — an official program of lay indoctrination was put in motion, entailing the creation of an extensive literature, in Latin and in England's vernaculars, for propagating basic knowledge of the faith.[41] John Thompson has suggested that Maidstone's psalms, like the later 1414 paraphrase of the same psalms by Thomas Brampton, may have been conceived and written precisely for the kind of bundled circulation with other brief vernacular items on doctrinal basics in which it does occur.[42] Twenty-seven copies of

---

[39] See Edden, *Richard Maidstone's Penitential Psalms*, p. 12; see also Edden's paper, "Richard Maidstone's *Penitential Psalms*," *Leeds Studies in English* n.s. 17 (1986), 77–94.

[40] Eamon Duffy, *The Stripping of the Altars: Traditional Religion in England c.1400–c.1580*, pp. 54, 61.

[41] See, for example, William of Pagula's *Oculus sacerdotis* and John Mirk's English verse *Instructions for Parish Priests* based on it, the *Lay Folks' Catechism* deriving from Thoresby's constitutions, and so on, including Maidstone's penitential psalms paraphrase and the cognate vernacular religious writings with which it circulated.

[42] John J. Thompson, "Literary Associations of an Anonymous Middle English Paraphrase of Vulgate Psalm L," especially p. 45. The invention and circulation of this literature of indoctrination has been variously discussed; see especially Leonard E. Boyle, "The *Oculus Sacerdotis* and Some Other Works of William of Pagula"; G. H. Russell, "Vernacular Instruction of the Laity in the Later Middle Ages in England: Some Texts and Notes"; Vincent Gillespie, "*Doctrina* and *Predicacio*: The Design and Function of Some Pastoral Manuals"; and Anne Hudson, "A New Look at the Lay Folks' Catechism," especially pp. 243–45. The crucial contribution on its social function is Thomas N. Tentler, "The *Summa for Confessors* as an Instrument of Social Control"; also the general remarks in Tentler's later *Sin and Confession on the Eve of the Reformation*, especially pp. xiii–xxi; and Lee W. Patterson, "The 'Parson's Tale' and the Quitting of the 'Canterbury Tales.'" The practical work of the church in promoting an ideal

various redactions of Maidstone's penitential psalms survive, all of them in manuscripts comprising collections of cognate doctrinal and devotional vernacular writings, the commonest in circulation with Maidstone's work being *The Prick of Conscience*.[43]

"Popular piety seems here to have absorbed and interiorized clerical objectives without any sense of incongruity," concludes Duffy.[44] In fact, the contemporary "sense of incongruity" seems to have been acute in this area; there was considerable popular objection to the impositions of confession and the aggrandizement of priestly power that came with it, as propagated by such writings as Maidstone's psalms. The Lollard agitation against problems associated with this sacrament was extensive; for example, one of the Lollard "Twelve Conclusions" of c. 1395 made just this point:

> the articlis of confession that is sayd necessari to salvaciun of man, with a feynid power of absoliciun enhaunsith prestis pride and yevith hem opertunite of privi calling . . . . Thei seyn that thei ben commissariis of God to deme of every synne, to foulin and to clensin qwom so thei lyke. Thei seyn that thei han the keys of hevene and of helle; thei mown cursyn and blissin, byndin and unbyndin at here owne wil, in so miche that for a busschel of qwete or xii.d be yere thei welen selle the blisse of hevene.[45]

Maidstone was active not only in promoting sacramental orthodoxy, but also in direct anti-Lollard activities. Among the works imputed to him by Bale is a tract *Contra Wiclevistas*, though it is not known to survive.[46] Maidstone, however, also involved himself in anti-Lollard agitation at Oxford, specifically in public controversy with John Ashwardby, vicar of St. Mary the Virgin (the university church of Oxford), over a period of some months at some indeterminate point between 1384 and 1395, possibly c. 1392.[47] Tellingly, and as is characteristic of such cases, Ashwardby's contributions do not survive; his provocations are known only through the reports of them in Maidstone's hostile reactions: a longer, earlier tract, *Protectorium pauperum*, eventually copied into the *Fasciculi Zizaniorum*, the Carmelite

---

of social order and enforcing it is emphasized by Sylvia L. Thrupp, "Social Control in the Medieval Town."

[43] The manuscript contexts in which Maidstone's psalms occur are summarized in Edden, *Richard Maidstone's Penitential Psalms*, pp. 12–20.

[44] Duffy, *The Stripping of the Altars*, p. 265.

[45] The quotation is from Anne Hudson, ed., *Selections from English Wycliffite Writings*, p. 27.

[46] Bale lists Maidstone's writings in the *Illustrium maioris Britanniae scriptorum summarium* ([Wesel: D. van der Straten, 1548] *STC* 1295), fols. 172v–173r, and the *Index Britanniae Scriptorum*, p. 355.

[47] The controversy is noticed, with discussion of its contexts, in Jeremy I. Catto, "Wyclif and Wycliffism at Oxford 1356–1430," p. 229.

dossier of anti-Lollard documentary tools;[48] and a briefer, more focusedly acerb polemic, *Determinacio contra Magistrum Johannem vicarium ecclesie Sancte Marie Oxoniensis*, in which reference is made to the *Protectorium*.[49]

Evidently, Ashwardby, a secular, had formed doubts about the sort of mendicancy espoused by Maidstone and others similarly placed. Trouble came when Ashwardby voiced such doubts in his public preaching. Moreover, he took to preaching on the dubieties of mendicancy "in Anglicis [sc. verbis]" ["in English"], not "in scolis et coram clericis in lingua latina" ["in the schools for a clerical audience in Latin"], but "coram laicis in lingua materna" ["for a lay audience, in the mother-tongue"]. Ashwardby went so far as to advocate the position that it was wrong, even sinful, to give alms to mendicants, and argued furthermore that his auditors were bound to stop doing so. To the mendicant friar "est tribuendum, set quid?" ["giving is appropriate, but giving what?"]. Maidstone represents Ashwardby's position as "non elemosina corporalis, non cibum, non potus, non hospicium, set aspera increpacio et acuta correpcio, ut per hoc discat stultitiam suam, qui se obligavit ad huiusmodi mendicitatem" ["not bodily sustenance, nor food, nor drink, nor shelter, but sharp rebuke and strict correction, that the mendicant might come thereby to know his own stupidity, the stupidity that binds him to this sort of mendacity"].[50] In giving voice to such a position, Ashwardby aligned himself, provocatively in Maidstone's view, with those who "his diebus quidam evangelicae paupertatis et aemuli Christi pauperes voluntarios eleemosynis fidelium non debere sustentari docent et praedicant . . . multaque contra sanctos Christi ore blasphemo perstrepere non formidant" ["go about these days to teach and to preach that those who elect to be poor, in emulation of Christ and the evangelical poverty, ought not to be given sustenance . . . and they have no shame to croak out a good deal more besides, set against Christ's saints, with the voice of blasphemy"].[51]

Ashwardby used the argument that mendicancy was a variety of theft, Robin Hood in reverse, by which false mendicants "pauperes Christi suo vectu expoliant et defraudent" ["despoil and defraud Christ's own poor of their due"].[52] Alms-giving to representatives of such already wealthy ecclesiastical establishments as the fraternal orders effectively took

---

[48] A text is published in Arnold Williams, "*Protectorium Pauperis*, a Defense of the Begging Friars by Richard Maidstone, O. Carm. (d. 1396)." On the *Fasciculus*, see especially James Crompton, "*Fasciculi Zizaniorum*."

[49] A text of the *Determinacio* is published in Edden, "The Debate," pp. 120–34.

[50] Edden, "The Debate," p. 123. The circumstances in which such provocative preaching as Ashwardby's would have occurred are delineated in Simon Forde, "Nicholas Hereford's Ascension Day Sermon, 1382," pp. 205–10.

[51] Williams, "*Protectorium Pauperis*," p. 135, lines 28–33.

[52] Edden, "The Debate," p. 122.

charitable sustenance away from the truly needy, who suffered by consequence. Maidstone understood where such arguments might lead: to the undoing of pilgrimage and other forms of veneration of the saints, and to a wholesale despoiling of the church and even derogation of the donation of Constantine. From such views it followed

> quod praedia et possessiones datae collegiis et monasteriis possessionatis, archiepiscopis et episcopis etiam ad sustentationem clericorum et monachorum Deo servientium, essent malae collatae; oblationes etiam eleemosynae quae conferuntur a fidelibus et peregrinis ad aedificia basilicarum, et ad alios pios usus, ubi Domino servitur vel ubi imagines et corpora sanctorum martyrum venerantur, essent penitus inutiles et infructuosae. . . . et tandem concedet quod non est eleemosyna vel opus meritorium parochiano aliquid conferre suo rectori vel vicario corpore valido, ultra oblationes de consuetudine debitas et decimas iure taxatas; et finaliter quod eleemosyna quam contulit Constantinus Silvestro, quando dotavit ecclesiam, fuit potius demeritoria quam meritoria.

> [that bequests and belongings given colleges and possessionary monasteries, archbishops and bishops, even for the sustenance of clerks and monks serving God, are wrongfully given; that offeratory alms, given by church-goers and pilgrims — where the divine service is done, or the images and relics of the sainted martyrs are venerated — for construction work in churches and the like pious projects, are altogether useless and pointless; . . . in the end, he reveals that it is not alms-giving, nor any meritorious deed, to give anything at all to one's vicar or rector — be he of sound body — except the customarily obligatory offerings and such tithings as are justly levied; and finally that the alms-deed that Constantine made Sylvester, when he endowed the church, was rather derogatory than a credit to him.][53]

Maidstone's narrower, immediate response was to accuse Ashwardby and others of his views of theft in their turn. Their strictures were only invidious: "Ex his omnibus, ut mihi videtur, sufficienter declaratum est ad quantum errorem processit malitia quorundam modernorum docentium publice et praedicando sic: nulli des pecuniam vel denarium qui plures habet quam tu, nulli des cibum aut potum qui melius solet pasci quam tu, et sic de aliis" ["From all the evidence, it seems to me adequately clear how deeply into error will extend the malice of those of the moderns who are willing to teach publicly and to preach in such terms: 'Give cash or funding to no one who has more than you; give food and drink to no one who seems better fed than you'; and so forth"].[54] Maidstone represents the doubter as if saying to himself, "Video quod isti fratres habent meliores domus quam ego, meliora indumenta quam ego, meliores libros, et huiusmodi; video bene habundanciam eorum, set non video indigenciam, et quia videtur michi quod mendicant vbi non indigent, ideo corripio illos et increpo nec aliquid aliud

---

[53] Williams, "*Protectorium Pauperis*," pp. 140–41, lines 37–43 and 56–60.

[54] Williams, "*Protectorium Pauperis*," p. 143, lines 149–53.

dabo illis" ["'I see those friars living in better homes than I have, wearing better clothes than I do, having better books,' and so forth; 'clearly indeed do I see their wealth, but I see no indigence; wherefore I attack them and complain, nor will I ever give them anything more'"].[55] In dissuading pious laypersons from giving charity to friars ("immo hoc omnino in sermonibus suis et actibus conantur efficere ut seculares devoti, qui servis Dei ministrant necessaria vite, a sua devocione cessent et desinant" ["indeed, and this whole-heartedly, by their preachments and their practice, they try to see to it that such pious laypersons as look after the vital needs of God's servants leave off their devotion and desist"]), Ashwardby and his like were doing real harm:

Et propterea predicant v[i]ctum non debere dari, quia melius solet pasci quam tu, non vestitum, quia melius induitur quam tu, non hospicium quia meliorem habet domum quam tu, et sic de aliis, ut per subtraccionem elemosinarum non solum divites meritum perdant, set et Christi pauperes priventur vite necessariis, et sic miserabilius pereant quam pecora vel iumenta.

[Moreover, they preach that food ought not be given since he (i.e., the friar) seems better fed than you, nor clothing, since he is better dressed than you, nor shelter, since he has a better home than you, and so on and so forth, in order not only that the well-to-do might lose merit, but also that Christ's own poor should be deprived of the necessities of life and thereby die more wretched deaths than swine or cattle — all for the elimination of alms-giving.][56]

In addition to murdering friars all but directly, as Maidstone implies, Ashwardby had also to be held responsible for his intention to turn others likewise into "latrones et homicides et expoliatores ecclesiarum" ["thieves and killers and church-pillagers"], no different from Lollards:

Et ideo videtur michi, sicut et merito videri debet cuilibet advertenti, quod intencio doctoris mei [i.e., Ashwardby] et omnium sibi simil[i]um non est alia nisi ut persuasiones et predicaciones su[e] possint avertere animos fidelium, ita ut amplius non conferant fratribus elemosinas suas et sic per inediam et angustiam compellat eos ad apostasiam, sintque latrones et homicides et expoliatores ecclesiarum, sicut maior pars est hiis diebus omnium qui sunt de secta lollardorum.

[And so it seems to me — as it ought to anyone else who cares to consider the matter aright — that the purpose of this good doctor (i.e., Ashwardby) and all of the same ilk, is none other than that their arguments and exhortations should so pervert the hearts and minds of the faithful that they

---

[55] Edden, "The Debate," p. 128.
[56] Edden, "The Debate," p. 130.

15

would give alms to friars no more, in order that, through starvation and straightened circumstance, he might drive friars into apostasy, making them killers and thieves and church-pillagers, as are already, even now, the most part of all adherents of Lollardy.][57]

Maidstone does not directly call Ashwardby a Lollard. He accuses him of promoting views and courses of action espoused by Lollards and of using the sort of verbal equivocation resorted to by persons anticipating charges of heresy (whereby, "forte si coram inquisitore heretice pravitatis essent de tanto errore culpati, possent se excusare" ["if, perchance, they were to stand before an inquiry into heretical depravity, accused of such error, they find means for exculpating themselves"]).[58] Maidstone names Ashwardby's views *errores* repeatedly, a charged term with particular legal weight in the context: some of the views of Ashwardby singled out for refutation by Maidstone were officially condemned as *errores* by the 1382 Blackfriars Council.[59] For Maidstone, Ashwardby was unequivocally a *subversor fidei* ("Quis predicat ista, nisi subversor fidei?" ["who would preach such things except a subverter of the faith?"]):[60] Ashwardby's interventions were Lollard-like, both in his resorting to English for conducting his public doctrinal discussion and in the substance of what he had to say. Attacks on concentrations of temporal wealth in the established church's control were a fundamental aspect of the Lollard program, as was the related, broad-fronted assault on private religions as ultimately anti-social and exploitive.[61] The specific conjunction at which Ashwardby seems to have been aiming — by his critique of a specific form of private religion because it was a specific form of official churchly theft — was a weak link vulnerable to attack on several grounds.

Maidstone teases out these scarifying propensities of Ashwardby's positions, raising the specter of the Lollard menace the better to exorcise it. Also, he puts some effort into arguing scripture with Ashwardby, showing that, by light of authoritative canons of Biblical interpretation, Ashwardby's exegeses were wrong. As in his Biblical explications, so too in his refutation of Ashwardby generally: for Maidstone, as Valerie Edden has said, what mattered was authority.[62] The mendicancy that Maidstone defended was right because

---

[57] Edden, "The Debate," p. 131.

[58] Edden, "The Debate," p. 131.

[59] E.g., Edden, "The Debate," pp. 121–23 and 117.

[60] Williams, "*Protectorium Pauperis*," p. 144, line 169.

[61] Anne Hudson, *The Premature Reformation: Wycliffite Texts and Lollard History*, pp. 347–51.

[62] Edden, "The Debate," p. 113: "Maidstone has a very clear idea of the essential issue at stake, for whilst the subject of the debate is mendicancy, Maidstone properly identifies the essential area of disagreement as that of authority: the authority to be attached to different interpretations of scripture and the necessity of following the authority of the Church as embodied in Canon Law and papal bulls." The debt here to the work of W. Scott Blanchard on the history of intellectual freedom, e.g., most recently,

authority — popes and lesser officers of the hierarchy, fathers of the church and other saints, and the established tradition of church practice — said it was right: "quod non solum quattuor ordines mendicancium sunt approbati in iure communi et ab ecclesia in quantum sunt ordines, set in quantum sunt mendicantes; ita quod mendicitas eorum non solum est permissa ab ecclesia set eciam approbata, cuius oppositum in vulgari predicavit ad populum . . . doctor meus reverendus (i.e., Ashwardby)" ["that the four mendicant orders enjoy the approbation of common law and the church, not only inasmuch as they are orders, but also inasmuch as they are mendicant, so that their mendicancy is not just suffered by the church, but is indeed promoted — the very opposite of what is being preached, in English, to the folk, by the reverend good doctor (i.e., Ashwardby)"].[63] Those who would dissent from this view were criminals, subject to official anathema and the wrath of God and the saints:

> Preterea, inpedire mendicitatem fratrum prohibetur a sede apostolica sub optentu illius indulgencie que continetur in omni bulla sub clausula "Nulli igitur." Que quidem indulgencia non est aliud quam indignacio Dei omnipotentis et beatorum apostoli Petri et Pauli. Set omne tale est approbatum a sede apostolica, cuius impedimentum est prohibitum ab eadem. . . . Quicunque fratribus ipsis in predicacionibus, confessionibus, sepulturis et elemosinis mediate vel inmediate inpedimentum prestant sub anathematis vinculo innodati sunt.

> [Moreover, to hinder the mendicancy of friars is forbidden by the apostolic see, by provision of the indulgence specified for the papal bull as a whole under the clause "To none therefore." The indulgence is none other than the very wrath of omnipotent God above and the sainted apostles Peter and Paul. Indeed, all such enjoy the approbation of the Holy See, and any hinderance of the same is strictly forbidden. . . . Anyone who puts lets, direct or indirect, in the friars' way, in respect of their preaching, confessing, burying, or alms-taking activities, is bound by the strictest bonds of anathema.][64]

3. The *Concordia*

The poem that Richard Maidstone wrote on the metropolitan crisis of 1392 reports information about the royal entry that concluded it in greater detail than any other source. The poem is not primarily a report, however; like Maidstone's other writings, the poem is above all an ideologically driven literary intervention, produced at a particular moment, addressing a particular political circumstance. The nature of the audience it aims at is difficult to divine

---

"The Negative Dialectic of Lorenzo Valla: A Study in the Pathology of Opposition," should be evident.

[63] Edden, "The Debate," p. 132.

[64] Edden, "The Debate," p. 134.

— certainly clerical, certainly secular or secularizing, possibly even narrowly courtly or courtly-clerical, certainly not popular, though not exactingly learned either — but, be that as it may, the poem is propaganda. In certain respects (e.g., the anti-Lollard remarks put into King Richard's mouth), the agenda may be Carmelite or idiosyncratically Maidstonian; chiefly, though, its agenda is royalist. The poem engrosses royal power, apologizing for and promoting a peculiarly Ricardian notion of "peace," in the form of submission to royal authority, however willful or arbitrary it might show itself to be. This is the sense made by the poem of the key term in its title, *concordia*: blank authoritarianism.

3.1. The Pageantry

There are five additional witnesses — contemporary and credibly independent of one another — to the events in London of 21–22 August 1392. In order of circumstantiality of detail and evident nearness to the events, these are: (1) an epistolary report from an unnamed writer to an unspecified addressee in French prose, a copy of which was kept in the episcopal register of Durham; (2) a Latin prose account by the so-called Monk of Westminster in a passage of the so-called *Westminster Chronicle*'s continuous narration of events of the period 1381–94; (3) the Latin prose account in the *Chronicon* of Henry Knighton (d. 1396), again within a continuous narration; (4) the English prose account in the "Common Version" of the continuation of the *Brut* for the period 1377–1419; and (5) a less circumstantial, more distanced summary remark on events in Thomas Walsingham's *Historia anglicana* (albeit that, for explaining the background of the crisis, Walsingham is distinctly better informed).[65]

Helen Suggett suggested that the surviving French letter might reflect — or indeed might be — an official account of the London event, written and circulated with royal or governmental

---

[65] A text of each of these witnesses is supplied below, in Appendix 1. The account from the Middle English *Brut* is from the "Common Version to 1419" in the classification of Lister M. Matheson, *The Prose Brut: The Development of a Middle English Chronicle*, specifically from a manuscript of "The Common Version to 1419, ending 'in rule and governance': Group A (CV–1419[r&g]:A)," no. 36 in Matheson's list. For the qualities of the several texts as witnesses in general, see Antonia Gransden, *Historical Writing in England*, volume II: *C. 1307 to the Early Sixteenth Century* (London: Routledge & Kegan Paul, 1982). The notice of the pageantry in the continuation of the *Eulogium temporis*, though it supplies important background, is itself exiguous: "Postea Londonienses magnam summam auri collegerunt ita quod quidam propter illam collectam fugerunt de civitate. Et regem venientem cum maxima solempnitate tanquam angelum Dei susceperunt, tradideruntque sibi claves civitatis et in auro XL. ml. li. ei obtulerunt. Et sic regimen civitatis receperunt" (ed. Frank Scott Haydon, *Eulogium historiarum sive temporis*, Rolls Series 9, 3 vols. [London: Longmans, Brown, Green, Longmans and Roberts, 1863], 3.367–68).

sponsorship, to propagate news of the city's submission.[66] The letter's anonymous preservation, without named addressor or addressee, in the Durham episcopal register, as if an official document, lends weight to the suggestion, as might also the evidence for propagation of official accounts of other near contemporary news of state. The circulation of such reports of the "Good Parliament" of 1376, for example, and of the process of the "Merciless Parliament" of 1388 has been inferred from surviving chronicle accounts, though the most thoroughly studied cases date from the later period, 1397–99, of Richard II's tyranny and deposition.[67] Publicizing the king's victory of 1392 would have served a clear interest, and there may well have been an official effort to do so, possibly attested by the surviving letter. On the other hand, the pageantic entry itself already advertised the royal triumph publicly enough, and such agreements as there are among the surviving accounts may reflect direct witness to the civic events themselves, rather than the mediation of some shared documentary source. None would appear to have had access to private or restricted information.

Maidstone's poem and the other witnesses agree about the day's events, albeit there are intermittent omissions on the part of one or another of the sources. The returning monarch, with his queen, was first greeted near Wandsworth, by an extensive civic delegation: numerous representatives of the various city guilds, all distinctively liveried and posed together by guild, the twenty-four aldermen of the city, and the (royally appointed) warden, or *custos*. On their knees, the aldermen and *custos* here made presentation to the king of the sword of the city and its keys — with the warden addressing the king, and handling and handing over the symbolic tokens.

Somewhat nearer the city, the king was likewise greeted by an extensive delegation of the religious of the city — friars, monks, secular priests and clerks, boys, and even the bishop of London — singing the *Te Deum* and the *Summe Trinitati*.

At Bridgegate, following speeches of welcome on behalf of the aldermen and the whole corporation, the warden made presentation to the king of two great horses, trapped with cloth of gold and parti-colored red and white fabric, with saddles of silver, and to the queen of a great palfrey, similarly trapped, with a saddle of gold.

At the entry into Fish Street, two handsome young men with gold thuribles honored the king by censing him.

---

[66] Helen Suggett, "A Letter Describing Richard II's Reconciliation with the City of London, 1392," pp. 210–11.

[67] See especially Given-Wilson, "Adam Usk, the Monk of Evesham and the Parliament of 1397–8," p. 333; also "The Manner of King Richard's Renunciation: A 'Lancastrian Narrative'?"; and George Osborne Sayles, "The Deposition of Richard II: Three Lancastrian Narratives." The broader historiographical perspective is provided by Gransden, "Propaganda in English Medieval Historiography."

At the Great Conduit in Cheapside, running with red wine for the occasion, king and queen were greeted by a choir posed atop the conduit structure, whence also maidens scattered gold coins; and a boy, costumed as an angel in white, offered them a drink from a gold cup.

Then beyond the Great Conduit, still in Cheap, had been erected — over the street, apparently, suspended by ropes — a great tower, from which descended, as if borne on clouds ("hors d'une nuwe" — Appendix 1, p. 91), two caroling angels, a boy and a girl, bringing gilt crowns of great cost, one for the king and one for the queen; with appropriate speeches, the *custos* crowned king and queen with the angels' gifts.

The procession continued along Cheap to the Little Conduit, where was posed a choir of caroling angels to greet the king, musicians and singers alike arranged in three ranks around an impersonation of the Trinity crowning the structure.

Then the king was met by a clerical procession issuing from St. Paul's that conducted him to the church door, where the king dismounted; there he entered and made offering at the tomb of the fabled bishop of London, St. Erkenwald.

At Ludgate, going out of the city proper, atop Temple Bar, was the representation of a wilderness, with appropriate flora and impersonations of a variety of fauna as well. In this setting was a figure recognizable as John the Baptist, who called out on seeing the king, "Agnus et ecce dei" ["Look, the Lamb of God" — line 372]. An angel or angels came down from this construction, with additional gifts from the city for the king and queen; with speeches again, the city *custos* presented a gilt-engraved tablet of the Crucifixion to the king and, to the queen, a gilt-engraved tablet of St. Anne, to whom she was specially devoted.

Processing on towards Westminster, the king and queen passed through crowds — especially thick at the Savoy, according to one source — along a route decorated with paintings and images, as well as banners and draperies of cloth of gold, silk, and double-dyed fabrics.

From Westminster Abbey issued another clerical procession of greeting, which conducted king and queen into the abbey for an elaborate service (described in detail by the Monk of Westminster, who would have been a participant).

Then at Westminster palace, the king, who had by now been riding all day, was ceremonially redressed, "en une longe gowne" (Appendix 1, p. 91), and enthroned in sight of the attendant citizenry. His queen, the archbishop of Canterbury, and the bishop of London, on their knees, imprecated the king's mercy on behalf of the city. In response, the king's forgiveness was publicly announced, and he was thanked officially for it in a final speech by the *custos*.

After drinking some wine and eating some spices, by way of refection after such labors, the king went on privately to sup at Kennington, and all departed.

The following day, again in the city proper, the city *custos* hosted a banquet honoring the king and queen, in the course of which the king was presented with a great dining table, silver and gilt enameled, nine feet long, and costing 500 marks, according to one of the sources, and, at the same time, the queen was presented with a hanaper of beryl and a ewer of gold.

3.2. Propaganda

As Gordon Kipling has pointed out, these 1392 events had the shape of a coronation entry, as attested by a variety of roughly contemporary northern European examples, which all took their meaning, broadly, in Kipling's view at least, from the parallel scriptural model of Christ's Easter-season entry into Jerusalem.[68] Though Maidstone does relatively little with the biblical matter the events supplied him, the pageantry did unequivocally equate King Richard with Jesus Christ the savior, most egregiously in the Ludgate tableau, with its John the Baptist figure pointing to Richard, calling out "Agnus et ecce dei" ["Look, the Lamb of God" — line 372]. Richard was favored on other occasions by the same sort of equation, with Christ as savior or Christ as martyr, and always with the same unscrupulous enlistment of piety in support of worldly political causes.[69]

The more immediate, specific parallel for the 1392 event, however, as Kipling also points out, was the actual coronation entry of King Richard in 1377. The 1377 entry followed the same route and employed some of the same pageants, most noteworthily perhaps at the Great Conduit, where, in 1377, on his way through the city, Richard had seen much the same business: the conduit running wine, "transfigured as the City of Heaven," where "Angels stood atop the four towers scattering gold leaves in his path and gold florins upon his person."[70] These parallels between the 1377 and 1392 entries may be regarded as reflecting a prudential economy on the part of the city. What had worked satisfactorily in 1377 could be made to serve again in 1392, without new investment; there may not have been ample time to prepare the 1392 entry, and the city did not have long or varied experience of staging such shows anyway; the exigent thing, given these circumstances, was repetition. At the same time, however, the repetition would inevitably have had specific exploitable symbolic gravities. By in effect crowning the king again in 1392, the city admitted that its antecedent reluctance to submit to the royal will was criminal, even insurrectionary. All of the city's concerns about its liberties, the franchise and the staples, royal and noble interference in civic political arrangements, and its own internal factional struggles, or aristocratic and royal extortion, were

---

[68] Gordon Kipling, "Richard II's 'Sumptuous Pageants' and the Idea of Civic Triumph."

[69] John M. Bowers, "*Pearl* in Its Royal Setting: Ricardian Poetry Revisited," especially pp. 144–45, and, on Richard's uses for the John the Baptist figure, pp. 122–36. Maria Wickert, *Studien zu John Gower*, p. 172, connects this evidence for a Ricardian Baptist cult, including that of Maidstone's poem, with matter in John Gower's (tellingly named) *Vox clamantis*. See also Saul, *Richard II*, p. 385, and John Taylor, "Richard II's Views on Kingship," pp. 194–97.

[70] Kipling, "Richard II's 'Sumptuous Pageants,'" p. 88; Appendix 2, below, gives the two detailed contemporary accounts of the 1377 entry. On the developments of this form of English civic pageantry generally, see also Kipling, "Triumphal Drama: Form in English Civic Pageantry."

impertinent here. By its insubordination, the city had effectively dethroned its rightful king; now, properly servile, the city tried to make good its malfeasance by crowning him king again.

The medieval royal entries into London as a whole constitute speech "about power," as Lawrence M. Clopper has concluded, in which "the monarch and his court usurp the city to act out their social drama. The action is exclusionary even though it is intended through display and majesty to create a bond between the ruler and the ruled."[71] Though the 1392 royal entry in particular deployed scriptural references and schemes, it was still fundamentally political, "about power," rather than spiritual or religious; and it was the political and social import of the symbolic events that Maidstone particularly developed in the poem he wrote for the occasion. As a repetition of the 1377 coronation entry, Maidstone's representation of the 1392 event had parallels also with other historical political spectacles, such as the ancient Roman *triumphus* or, more precisely, with the imperial *adventus*.[72] Though the events themselves seem to have done little with such parallels, Maidstone amplified them. For example, he describes the mayor and aldermen as toga-wearing senators, explaining their role in civic governance in these terms: "Iure senatorio, urbs hiis regitur quasi Roma" ["Like Rome, the city's ruled by them, as senators" — line 73]; later Richard, having entered the city on horseback avowedly like a "Caesar," line 200 (compare line 431), mounts a tribunal ("nitidum scandit . . . tribunal" — line 461) to address the thronging crowds. These parallels might tend to make Richard a Marius or a Sulla or some other antique *dictator* or *imperator* returning to Rome with an army at his back and proscriptions in prospect, though Maidstone does not take things so far.

In other ways as well, Maidstone shapes the material provided him by events to engross King Richard's authority. Most important is the structure Maidstone imparted to his whole poem by the ending he put on it. All other sources of information about the 1392 entry include description of the concluding banquet, at which the king and queen were given, appropriately, an ornate dining table and elaborate vessels for serving. In the end, Richard and the city oligarchs sat together and dined. The epistolary report (nearest an official account) describes the conjoint festal celebrations as extending into the night, with the king accompanied on his way home from the city banqueting hall to his palace at Westminster by crowds of common well-wishers, who were invited into the palace to share a final goodnight drink with the king.[73]

---

[71] Lawrence M. Clopper, "The Engaged Spectator: Langland and Chaucer on Civic Spectacle and the *Theatrum*," pp. 131–32.

[72] Kipling, "Richard II's 'Sumptuous Pageants,'" p. 92, and compare "Triumphal Drama," pp. 38–41 and 47–50.

[73] See Appendix 1.1, below.

The symbolic valence of such banqueting — widely developed by Shakespeare, for example, in the "interrupted banquet" scene of *The Tempest* (3.3) — is specific. It stands for social harmony. Eating together can even have egalitarian implications, serving as a reminder that, all the evidences of inequality notwithstanding, within the human community all still share basic needs, king and commoner alike. But this was not the type of *concordia* that Maidstone wished to affirm. He omits the banquet. Maidstone's poem ends instead with the king's enthronement and the speech of dire warning pronounced thence. The concluding image with which Maidstone leaves his readers is not the banquet, but this impersonal *tableau vivant* of a hierophant enthroned on a dais, freighted with other distancing emblems of regal authority, scarcely human at all, but above all the divinized vessel ("Agnus et ecce dei" ["Look, the Lamb of God" — line 372]) of an implacable power to which mortals were bound to submit, recognizing in him the inhabitation of this extraordinary and supernatural something. Maidstone's poem provided the king "a portrait of himself as triumphant over the powers of both time and of rebellion," Lynn Staley comments, "in a way that is emphatically ceremonial, formal, hieratic, and at a far remove from the festive mode;"[74] and there is other evidence for Richard's repeated use of such hieratic self-presentations for attempting to intimidate the people around him. The *Eulogium*-continuator has information about his manner at crown-wearings:

Rex in diebus solennibus in quibus utebatur de more regalibus jussit sibi in camera parari thronum, in quo post prandium se ostentans sedere solebat usque ad vesperas, nulli loquens sed singulos aspiciens. Et cum aliquem respiceret, cuiuscumque gradus fuerit, oportuit ipsum genuflectere.

[On solemn occasions, on which it was his habit to put his insignia of royalty to use, the king ordered a throne to be set up for him in his rooms, on which he would then sit, from after dinner until vespers, making display of his person, speaking to none but studying them all. When his gaze attached to someone, that person was expected to kneel to the king, there and then, no matter his rank.][75]

The image from the 1392 entry with which Maidstone ends his poem is the same sort of real-life repetition of the Westminster portrait of King Richard that the *Eulogium* also describes, done in flesh and cloth and furniture.[76] Evidently, the king himself did not even speak on the 1392 occasion, instead holding himself beyond direct communication; his threats were

---

[74] Lynn Staley, "Gower, Richard II, Henry of Derby, and the Business of Making Culture," p. 80.

[75] *Eulogium*, ed. Haydon, 3.378; see also Saul, "Richard II and the Vocabulary of Kingship," especially pp. 854 and 875.

[76] On the portraiture, see especially Selby Whittingham, "The Chronology of the Portraits of Richard II."

delivered through the mouth of a royal officer, as if the words of the living god speaking through an empty oracular vessel.[77]

The sequence of gift-givings leading up to this point, in the London pageant as in Maidstone's representation of it, prepares for the climactic image of authority's need for submission: first, the keys to the city (inevitably a reminder, post-Freud, also of a more basic kind of power over others than that coming of access to a city by its gates) and a sword, its point at the throat of the mayor ("ad instar / Tristis captivi" ["Just like a prisoner, / With woeful face" — lines 134–35]) and, by extension, at the throats of the aldermen kneeling with him and the whole city (lines 132–53);[78] then richly trapped and saddled horses (brute force, in other words) readied for submission to the king's and queen's control ("Dantur in hoc signum," as Maidstone's *custos* explains, "quod se reddunt modo cives: / Corpora, divicias, Pergama, queque sua" ["They're given as a sign that Londoners now yield / Their bodies, riches, Pergamum, and all that's theirs" — lines 211–12]); then the crowns that conventionally give public evidence of authority (lines 289–316); and finally, the pious images of the crucified Christ Jesus and his grandmother St. Anne enjoining mercy and in doing so implying the real possibility of its opposite (lines 379–452).

The speeches accompanying the gift-givings in Maidstone's account — certainly fabricated by Maidstone though probably also reflecting something of what was actually said[79] — make

---

[77] This detail is supplied by the anonymous letter (Appendix 1.1, below) and by Knighton (Appendix 1.3, below) only; Maidstone puts his version of the speech in Richard's own mouth.

[78] On the keys and sword, see Sylvia Federico, "A Fourteenth-Century Erotics of Politics: London as a Feminine New Troy," pp. 145–46; also Michael Hanrahan, "'A Straunge Succesour Sholde Take Youre Heritage': The *Clerk's Tale* and the Crisis of Ricardian Rule," pp. 345–46.

[79] Verbal parallels with the other sources tend to suggest that the speeches reported in Maidstone's poem may not be altogether his own fabrications. Possibly some kind of official written report of the London event was available to some or all of those whose writings about it survive, though each writer would have used this hypothetical official source differently. For example, compare the *Concordia* lines 132–39: "Accessit propius custos, secumque togati; / Claves leva manus, dextra tenet gladium, / Ad se converso puncto mucronis; ad instar / Tristis captivi, sic sua verba refert: / 'En, rex, cuius ut est nimium metuenda potestas, / Sic et amanda nimis, nec reverenda minus: / En, humiles cives, vestris pedibus provoluti, / Reddunt se vobis et sua cunta simul'" and the French epistolary report (Appendix 1.1): "Le gardeyn porta en sa mayn un espé, et le pomel en haut et la point en sa mayn, et lez clyeffs de la ville, et qant ills furent devant le Roy, le gardeyn disoyt, genulant luy et sez compaignons, 'Mon seignur liege, si sont voz lieges, qe se mettent en vostre grace et mercy lour vies et corps et toutz lour bienz, en requirant vostre grace et mercy.'" See further above, pp. 19–20. On the implication of such evidence for the question of whether or not the 1392 speeches were properly scripted, as for a theatrical performance, see Gordon Kipling, "The London Pageants for Margaret of Anjou: A Medieval Script Restored," especially pp. 6 and 25n8.

repetitions of this basic sequence of civic submission and royal acquiescence. At Wandsworth, the *custos* represents London's citizenry as prostrate: "En, humiles cives, vestris pedibus provoluti, / Reddunt se vobis et sua cunta simul" ["Behold: your humble citizens, beneath your feet / Surrender all they have and their own selves to you" — lines 139–40]; "Acceptamus," the king replies, "tam vos quam reddere vestrum" ["We take you in, and your surrender, willingly" — line 150]. Again at Bridgegate, having already pointed out "quod se reddunt modo cives: / Corpora, divicias, Pergama, queque sua" ["that Londoners now yield / Their bodies, riches, Pergamum, and all that's theirs" — lines 211–12], the *custos* adds: "In vestris manibus sit eorum vitaque morsque, / Et regat ad libitum regia virga suos" ["Their life and death is now to be within your hands, / And may your royal rod guide subjects at its will" — lines 213–14]; the king, "contentus ad hec" ["at this contented" — line 215], replies: "Concedimus pacem genti que restat in urbe" ["We grant our peace to those that live within these walls" — line 217]. In Cheapside, giving the two crowns, the *custos* asserts that the *plebs* of the city "Mittit et hinc, binas vobis referendo coronas, / Innumeras grates, si capiatis eas" ["And so they send to you, by giving these two crowns, / Their countless thanks, if you will kindly take this gift" — lines 305–06]; "Contentantur ad hec," Maidstone reports, "tam rex quam regia coniux; / Subridendo parum sumit uterque datum" ["At this the king and royal bride are well content; / And, smiling slightly, each one takes their gift in turn" — lines 309–10]. At Ludgate, the *custos* voices the hope that "regis et ira cadit" ["the royal wrath / Subsides" — lines 407–08] now that the king sees the city's submission in the gifts it gives, "In signum pacis quam rogat hic populus" ["To signify the peace which all your people beg" — line 420]; the king replies, "Sponte remitto mee crimina cunta plebis" ["I grant forgiveness gladly for my people's crimes" — line 426].

These repetitions culminate in the speech from the throne with which Maidstone ends his poem. On behalf of the city, the queen again offers submission and begs for mercy (lines 463–92).[80] The response is, first of all, a justification of the royal wrath: the city's degeneracy required it (lines 499–512). The same perverse rationale is echoed in Walsingham, who says of the citizens, when they had declined to give the king the money his profligacies required,

> erant quippe tunc inter omnes fere nationes gentium elatissimi, arrogantissimi, et avarissimi, ac male creduli in Deum et traditiones avitas, Lollardorum sustentatores, religiosorum detractores, decimarum detentores, et communis vulgi depauperatores. In tantum excrevit eorum supercilium, ut auderent leges condere, quibus adventantes de circumjacentibus villis et provinciis, contra rationem omnem humanum, Deum, et justitiam, molestarent, gravarent, et fatigarent. Praetereo

---

[80] For Anne's part in events, see Paul Strohm, "Queens as Intercessors" (in *Hochon's Arrow: The Social Imagination of Fourteenth-Century Texts*), pp. 107–11, and Federico, "A Fourteenth-Century Erotics of Politics," pp. 151–52; on Anne's part in Ricardian culture in general, see Andrew Taylor, "Anne of Bohemia and the Making of Chaucer."

eorum inhumanitatem, sileo rapacitatem, reticeo infidelitatem, transeo malignitatem, quam indisciplinate in adventantes populos exercuerunt. Qui si vellem cuncta describere quae perpetraverunt hoc tempore, librum scriberem qui foret, horresco.

[Of all peoples (almost), the Londoners were then indeed the most arrogant, self-important, and avaricious, putting little faith in God and His venerable ways; they were supporters of the Lollards, critics of the religious, tithings-witholders, and general despoilers of the folk. So puffed up was their pride that they made it a matter of law — in the face of all human reason, of God, and of justice itself — to harrass, to burden, and so to grind down all who came there from outlying towns and provinces. They behaved themselves towards those who came to London with such callousness — their inhumanity, I pass over; as to their rapacity, I keep still; of their faithlessness, best not speak; and their malice, let that go too. But it makes me shudder, to think on the book that I could write, were I willing to tell all of the criminality of which they were guilty at that time.][81]

The king is placated by the gifts given him and his queen's intercessions (lines 515–18). He requires the city to treat his nobility better than had been done lately ("Contemptu proceres non habetote meos" ["Don't scorn or hold my lords and nobles in contempt"] — line 520), as in the case of his treasurer, Bishop Waltham; to leave off supporting seditious religious dissent, as mentioned also by Walsingham ("Antiquam servate fidem. Nova dogmata semper / Spernite, que veteres non didicere patres" ["Observe the ancient law. Reject for evermore / New doctrines that the ancient fathers did not learn"] — lines 521–22); and to respect the ecclesiastical hierarchy, the regular orders especially ("Non habet illa [i.e., ecclesia] gradum, quin colat ipse deum" ["It has no sacred rank that does not worship God"] — line 524). He restores the city's "rights," albeit his doing so makes it clear that these are not properly rights but only his royal pleasure (lines 531–36); and he enjoins persistent fear of the royal wrath. Fear is peace, he says; the absence of fear will bring trouble and destruction:

Sit et in urbe mea bona pax — contencio nulla,
   Nec conventiculum federis insoliti.
Si nostras etenim rumor penetraverit aures
   Obvius hiis monitis, urbs luet — haud dubium!

[And in my city let there be fair peace — not strife,
   And no newfangled gatherings in novel leagues.
If any news should reach me that conflicts with this
   Advice, the city will regret it — mark my words!] (Lines 527–30)

---

[81] Thomas Walsingham, *Thomae Walsingham, quondam monachi S. Albani, historia anglicana*, ed. Henry Thomas Riley, Rolls Series 28.1, 2 vols. (London: Longman, Green, Longman, Roberts, and Green, 1863–64), 2.208.

Introduction

Maidstone's *Concordia* is an apology for this perverse notion, which, as Nigel Saul has argued, was characteristically Ricardian. "In Richard's hands it was turned into a doctrine almost absolutist in tone":

> Richard saw the principal object of his government as the establishment of what he referred to as "peace" — unity, in other words — in his realm. And, following Giles [of Rome's *De regimine principum*], he believed that he could only achieve this if he, the king, was strong and his subjects were obedient to his will. . . . Unity — that is, peace — was incompatible with dissent; what the king required was unquestioning acceptance of his rule and submission to his will.[82]

The term comes up repeatedly in the *Concordia*, and always in this peculiar sense: that "pax tribuetur" ["then will peace be yours" — line 54] is the city's initial hope; "Nil nisi pax petitur vestra" ["We seek for nothing but your peace" — line 204], the king is implored; the city's final gift-giving ("In signum pacis quam rogat hic populus" ["To signify the peace which all your people beg" — line 420]) evokes a royal promise of "pax . . . huic urbi, civibus atque meis" ["Let there be peace to London and my citizens" — line 422] but only as long as no rumor of "contencio" ["strife"] breaching "bona pax" ["fair peace" — line 527] reaches the king.

The concord within the city — evoked in Maidstone's poem in his descriptions of the cooperation of all the guilds and all their members in planning and performing the pageant, despite the recently violent, even revolutionary struggle within the city over democratic constitutional reforms; the concord between the city and the Ricardian aristocracy, enjoined in the final royal speech in Maidstone, despite recent violent struggle here too; the concord between the city and the king himself, likewise recently disrupted — all depends on submission to the royally-imposed peace. There is no compromise, even of a sort that would allow for different degrees of power among the elements. Concord means only submission to authority. Such concord, being oppression, could not last, of course. Maidstone's representation is pure ideological myth-making, in Roland Barthes' sense: the poem treats as natural and inevitable something that was, in fact, not natural at all, but a product of particular local historical struggles.[83] But Maidstone was not writing history or satire; his was the ideologue's job, of making propaganda.

---

[82] Saul, *Richard II*, pp. 387, 250, and 388; see also pp. 248–50, 376–77, and especially 385–88. Though no persistent Ricardian himself, John Gower was yet an articulate proponent of this Ricardian notion of "peace," e.g., in the *Confessio Amantis* Prol.141–53, concluding "For alle resoun wolde this, / That unto him which the heved is / The membres buxom scholden bowe" (lines 151–53). See John Gower, *Confessio Amantis*, vol. 1, ed. Russell A. Peck (Kalamazoo, MI: Medieval Institute Publications, 2000).

[83] Roland Barthes, *Mythologies*, trans. Annette Lavers, second ed. (London: J. Cape, 1972), pp. 142–45.

Concordia facta inter regem et cives Londonie

In his account of the entry, Maidstone incorporated three unscripted occurrences. Presumably selected from amongst numerous such accidents that would have occurred during the course of the day, they were included, not for the sake of reportorial comprehensiveness, but again because they could be made to serve Maidstone's agenda. Maidstone groups his descriptions of two of the three accidents together, as a kind of interlude, following his account of the initial extramural greetings at Wandsworth; the third is inset between the Bridgegate greeting, still outside the city, and the intramural series of fabulous set-pieces to follow; all three accidents are prelude-like announcements of the themes of the main pageant series.

First is a remark about the weather (lines 177–82): a squall of rain saddened the crowd, but it passed quickly by and then "Aura serena micat" ["The atmosphere shone bright" — line 182]. In the reaction of the crowd ("tunc sexus uterque / Turbari metuens turbine tam valido" ["and man and wife / Feared lest they be upset by such a raging storm" — lines 179–80]), Maidstone evokes the fear of King Richard that animated the civic pageantry in general and that would figure prominently in the royal speech concluding his poem; of the weather's clearing, Maidstone makes a comforting point, indirectly, about the king's clemency: "urbs modo nil trepidat" ["the city now was calm" — line 182].

Another of the accidents is more difficult for Maidstone to allegorize. A decorated cart carrying members of the royal entourage tipped over during the procession: a Phaeton must have been driving, Maidstone comments (lines 247–54). People laugh at the discomfiture of others putting on such airs; such accidents remind of common humanity, despite attempts at its denial, and naturally call for celebration, however small. Maidstone's suggestion, though, is that the common laughter was prompted more specifically by sight of the inadvertently bared thighs of one of the tumbled passengers, all of whom were women, he claims, as if what people found really funny was women's public embarrassment. Maidstone's remark might be put down to some commonplace clerical rage, except that Maidstone goes a step further, allegorizing the accident as a morality about the end of degeneracy and erotic indulgence: "Casus et ille placet, veniat (rogo) quod michi signat, / Corruat ut luxus et malus omnis amor" ["So may this lucky fall's significance come true, / And lechery and lustful passion come to grief" — lines 253–54]. Historically, of course, the complaint widely current at the time had to do with the indulgence in *luxus* and *malus amor* characteristic of Richard and the male company he kept; most famously, Walsingham complained of them:

Et hi nimirum milites plus erant Veneris quam Bellonae, plus potentes in thalamo quam in campo, plus lingua quam lancea viguerunt, ad dicendum vigiles, ad faciendum acta martia somnolenti.

[But these were knights rather more devoted to Venus than to Bellona, more potent in bed than on the battlefield, mightier of tongue than of lance, full of talk but then rather quiet when it came to actually doing anything war-like.][84]

Maidstone's allegorical labors over the tipped pageant car make some trivializing acknowledgment of such criticism, and then also, more to the point, turn the criticism away from Richard, arguing implicitly that, though immoral *luxus* may have been abroad in the kingdom in some form (here, courtly women) and was bound to be thrown down, it had nothing to do with the king himself, who, as his concluding speech makes clear, had come back to the city precisely in order to root out such degeneracy.[85]

The other accident Maidstone admits to his account is the most telling thematically. In Southwark, a banished homicide put himself in the king's way, throwing himself prostrate in front of the king's horse (lines 185–90). The homicide begs pardon of the king, and the king grants it him, there and then, and Maidstone moralizes: "Sicque pium miseri miseret solitum misereri, / Gracia quam tribuit restituatur ei!" ["Thus, kindly, he bestows his kindness on this wretch. / So may the grace that he has shown be shown to him!" — lines 189–90].

Like the weather, this incident too may be taken to hold predictive value for the city: the king was inclining towards mercy. A corollary implication would be that the city must have been as acknowledgedly guilty as the prostrating convict. Beyond the immediate allegorical value the episode had, for characterizing relations between the city and the king, the episode also makes a broader point — the point of the whole poem, in fact — about the nature of King Richard's sovereign power. It is absolute. The king might behave as if he were above and beyond any law, excepting his own will. He is reported to have said as much himself at the time. Regarding the law as being in his own heart and mouth licensed him to do anything he wanted:

[Ricardus] rex, nolens justas leges et consuetudines regni sui servare seu protegere, sed secundum arbitrium suae voluntatis facere quidquid desideriis suis occurrerit, . . . dixit expresse, vultu austero et protervo, quod leges suae erant in ore suo, et aliquotiens, in pectore suo, et quod ipse solus posset mutare et condere leges regni sui.

---

[84] In the *Chronicon Angliae, ab anno domini 1328 usque ad annum 1388, auctore monacho quodam Sancti Albani*, ed. Edward Maunde Thompson, Rolls Series 64 (London: Longman and Co., 1874), pp. 375–76; see Patricia J. Eberle, "The Politics of Courtly Style at the Court of Richard II," pp. 168–72, and Saul, *Richard II*, pp. 332–33. The sole contemporary apology for the Ricardian excess is given below, in Appendix 3.

[85] This episode is also discussed in Strohm, "Queens as Intercessors," p. 108n12; and Federico, "A Fourteenth-Century Erotics of Politics," p. 151.

Concordia facta inter regem et cives Londonie

[King Richard, not wishing to uphold or dispense the rightful laws and customs of the realm, but preferring to act according to his own arbitrary will and to do whatever he wished, . . . declared expressly, with an austere and determined expression, that the laws were in his mouth, or, at other times, that they were in his breast; and that he alone could change or make the laws of his kingdom.][86]

The cruelties and capricious malfeasance of his tyranny late in the reign are most often cited in evidence of these absolutist ambitions; in fact, his clemencies made the same point. In a brief article devoted to repairing Richard's bad odor in these respects, called "King Richard II of England: A Fresh Look," George Osborn Sayles cites the monarch's spontaneous pardon of a petty palace thief as an instance of his mansuetude, to be set against contemporary episodes of cruelty:

A thief was caught red-handed in Westminster Hall and sentenced to be hanged. And while the deputy marshal of the King's Bench "was in the process of executing the judgment, the king happened to pass by and he ordered him by word of mouth to delay execution." Shortly afterwards the culprit received a royal pardon.[87]

But this anecdote too, like his pardon of the Southwark homicide mentioned in Maidstone's 1392 poem, bespeaks the greater danger about Richard, or his greater glory, depending on one's perspective: in such "arbitrary gestures of grace," as Andrew Galloway has said, "proffered through and as sheer power," Richard's "pity" too becomes "an expression of

---

[86] The passage is from the sixteenth of the deposition articles, here quoted from the text of the articles incorporated verbatim in Walsingham's "Annales Ricardi Secundi et Henrici Quarti," ed. Henry Thomas Riley, in *Johannis de Trokelowe et Henrici de Blandeforde monachorum S. Albani, necnon quorundam anonymorum Chronica et annales regnantibus Henrico Tertio, Edwardo Primo, Edwardo Secundo, Ricardo Secundo, et Hernrico Quarto*, Rolls Series 28.3 (London: Longmans, Green, Reader, and Dyer, 1866), p. 267; trans. Given-Wilson, *Chronicles of the Revolution 1397–1400: The Reign of Richard III*, pp. 177–78. See also Saul, *Richard II*, p. 249.

[87] Sayles, "King Richard II of England: A Fresh Look," p. 31n19. Compare the remarks of Jacques Derrida, *On Cosmopolitanism and Forgiveness*, trans. Mark Dooley and Michael Hughes (London: Routledge, 2001), pp. 45–47, on "the right of grace," as discussed by Kant: "The absolute monarch can, by divine right, pardon a criminal; that is to say, exercise in the name of the State a forgiveness that transcends and neutralizes the law. Right beyond the law. . . . Wherever the harms concern the subjects themselves, which is to say almost always, the right of grace could not be exercised without injustice. In fact, one knows that it is always exercised in a conditional manner, in the function of an interpretation or a calculation on the part of the sovereign regarding what joins a particular interest (his own, those of his family, or those of a fraction of society) and the interest of the state." Invariably, it seems, Richard II mismanaged such calculations.

power."[88] By being kind as much as or more than by being cruel, he made manifest the absoluteness of his power. He might do anything he wanted, the greater the range of his doings — the more unpredictable and arbitrary they were — the more absolute his power. The literary job of Maidstone's *Concordia* is to illustrate and aggrandize this absolute power.

4. Text and Language

The *Concordia* survives in a single copy, as part of an acephalous manuscript now kept in the Bodleian Library, Oxford, shelf-marked *e Musaeo* 94 (*SC* 3631). It consists of twelve parchment folios (with two modern flyleaves), measuring 28 x 20.5 cms, now numbered 1–12, though an earlier foliation, running 121–32, is still visible. It is written throughout in a single hand, an *anglicana formata* of c. 1400, in a black ink, with headings in red and intermittent drawn large capitals in blue, the writing covering an area measuring 24 x 17 cms, framed and ruled uniformly for two columns per page, of forty-eight lines each. John Bale (1495–1563) had it at one point, though nothing of its provenance is otherwise known until its bequest by Gerard Langbaine (1609–58) to the Bodleian, where it has remained since.[89] The manuscript's surviving contents are as follows:

1. A concluding section of Maidstone, *Protectorium Pauperis* (inc. "quod non; si sit persona privata, dicit quod sic, dum"), the whole of which was edited by Williams (see above, note 48) from Oxford, Bodleian Library MS *e Musaeo* 86 (*SC* 3629), the so-called *Fasciculi Zizaniorum*, including collation of what survives of Maidstone's work in this manuscript, fols. 1r–5r.

2. Maidstone, *Determinacio contra Magistrum Johannem vicarium ecclesie Sancte Marie Oxoniensis* complete (inc. "Utrum Christus enumerans in evangelio pauperes, claudos"), as edited by Edden (see above, note 49), fols. 5r–8v.

3. Maidstone, *Concordia* complete, fols. 8v–11v.

4. Richard Lavenham, *Excerpciones a libro Tullii De natura deorum* complete (inc. "Tullius libro primo de natura deorum qui liber sic incipit"), which (to my knowledge) has not been published and is not attested by other copies, fols. 11v–12r. A page prepared for writing, though left blank, follows, fol. 12v.

---

[88] Andrew Galloway, "The Literature of 1388 and the Politics of Pity in Gower's *Confessio amantis*," p. 93; also pp. 92–96.

[89] The manuscript was already acephalous when Bale used it: see Crompton, "*Fasciculi Zizaniorum*," pp. 156–57.

The contents that survive suggest that the complete manuscript may have been a collection of Maidstone's writings, complete or at least extensive. Bale's lists of the writings of Maidstone that he had seen indicate Maidstone's literary corpus was once lengthy.[90] Alternatively, in light of the inclusion of Lavenham's Ciceronian *excerptiones*, the original whole may have been a collection of contemporary English Carmelite writings, including but not restricted to Maidstone's work. The *Fasciculi Zizaniorum* (also incorporating writings of both Lavenham and Maidstone) is evidence at least for contemporary Carmelite labors at literary preservation of this sort.

This evidence (such as it is) that the surviving manuscript is a compilation already suggests that the text of the *Concordia* in it is a redacted text, at some remove from an original presentation copy where the *Concordia* would have appeared by itself that would have been given the king or another patron, such as John of Gaunt, nearer the moment of the poem's occasion. Other evidence internal to the surviving copy of the *Concordia* corroborates this likelihood that the text we have derives from a second- or subsequent generation copy of Maidstone's poem.

First, the introductory lines 1–14, addressing someone who is both Maidstone's *socius* and namesake (line 10) — perhaps a Carmelite named Richard, like the Richard Lavenham whose own writing is represented in the same manuscript — suggest after-the-fact circulation for an audience other than the presumptive original royal or patronal audience.[91] The poem proper

---

[90] See above, note 46.

[91] Lavenham was a Carmelite, like Maidstone, and, again like Maidstone, he was connected by employment to the royal family: he was a confessor to Richard II. Moreover, in addition to the classicizing *Excerpciones ciceronianae* preserved in *e Musaeo* 94, Lavenham was also responsible for a brief catechetical English tract on the seven deadly sins (unpublished but surviving in London, British Library MS Royal 8.C.i, Harley 211, Harley 1197, and Harley 1288), akin to Maidstone's English penitential psalms. The congruence of interests and situations, combined with somewhat greater elevation and (possibly) seniority on Lavenham's part, would make Lavenham a likely recipient of a copy of Maidstone's *Concordia*, with a personalized verse address. Although it has been alleged that Lavenham was dead as early as 1381 or 1383, in fact he was still active as late as September 1399, so the date is no impediment. Finally, Lavenham was prior of the London Carmelite Convent (the capacity in which he acted in 1399), and, though the date at which he was elected is not attested, it is possible that he took some part in the 1392 London pageantry in an official capacity. On Lavenham, see Crompton, "*Fasciculi Zizaniorum*," pp. 164–65, and Paul Vincent Spade, "The Treatises *On Modal Propositions* and *On Hypothetical Propositions* by Richard Lavenham," especially pp. 49–50. A source of confusion about these introductory lines 1–14 has been that Maidstone and the Richard *socius* addressed in them (be he Lavenham or some other Richard) share their Christian name also with the king of England whose doings are the subject matter of the poem, engendering the notion that the *socius* addressed here was the king himself: this is the view that Smith espoused, "*Concordia Facta*," pp.

would originally have begun "M cape, ter quoque C, deciesque novem duo iunge," at what is now line 15, with the roman-numeral dating formula that occurs fairly widely as an opening in contemporary Latin poetry.[92] The surviving introductory lines 1–14 to Richard *socius* would have been added later, to address a specially prepared copy of the *Concordia* to this particular audience. Maidstone may have written other such introductions to cover copies addressed to others, though none are known to survive; other contemporary Anglo-Latin poems do survive, however, with multiple and interchangeable addresses.[93] These introductions would or may have been copied independently on separate sheets or new pages; the economical recopying that characterizes the surviving Bodleian manuscript would have led to the once distinctly introductory lines being crowded together with the rest of the poem proper. These considerations suggest that the copy of the *Concordia* in the Bodleian manuscript derives from a less formal, less official, less public copy that the author addressed to an intimate and equal, which that intimate subsequently made available for recopying into the surviving Bodleian manuscript compilation.

The interlined headings and marginalia of the surviving copy likewise appear to have been added later. In one case, a heading appears to be mistaken: "Hic dantur tabule domine regine eiusdem figure" (before line 429), i.e., of the same Crucifixion scene that was on the altarpiece given the king just before. The words of the *custos* in the poem itself (especially lines 445–50) imply that the altarpiece given the queen was of a different figure, of St. Anne, an implication

---

129–30 and 163, and it has been variously echoed (and might be inferred from Rigg, *History of Anglo-Latin Literature*, p. 285). That a person of Maidstone's situation would have addressed a monarch in the terms used in 1–14, especially a monarch possessed of the kind of extraordinary and frightened self-regard that characterizes Richard II, particularly during the 1390s, when the *Concordia* was written, is very difficult to conceive, the more so inasmuch as the rest of the poem's point is to elevate to all but divine stature the person ostensibly addressed so familiarly in 1–14. Wright, *Political Poems and Songs* 1.lxxiii, was right: the surviving copy of the poem derives from a text "addressed to a friend who was named like himself."

[92] Four of John Whethamstede's ten poems on the English civil wars (written 1455–61) begin with such dating formulas, for example; see David R. Carlson, "The Civic Poetry of Abbot John Whethamstede of St. Albans († 1465)," p. 234n89. The *Chronica tripertita* proper begins the same way ("Tolle caput mundi, C ter sex lustra fer illi, / Et decies quinque cum septem post superadde"), following Gower's preface (ed. Wright, *Political Poems and Songs* 1.417); another example ("Annis bis sex C, quater X bis ter, simul et C") is in Wright, *Political Poems and Songs* 1.52. The otherwise mystifying date in the explicit in the manuscript ("anno domini millesimo CCC. nonagessima tertio") might make sense as the date of the copy of the poem from which the *e Mus*. 94 copy was taken, rather than as the date of the poem's composition, which ought to have been late 1392.

[93] An example is the poem of Walter of Peterborough mentioned above, note 36: see Wright, *Political Poems and Songs* 1.97.

confirmed by another source, Knighton (see Appendix 1.3). In others, they are less helpful than might be expected (e.g., the heading before line 45 is premature, that before line 102 is belated, etc.) or idiosyncratic (e.g., there are marginal notes pointing to lists occurring in the poem next to lines 335–36 [musical instruments], 361–62 [trees], and 365–66 [beasts] but not next to lines 81 ff., where the poem's chief list occurs; the demeanor of king and queen is noted marginally next to lines 310–11, though nowhere else; etc.). The distribution of this matter in the surviving copy, as interlined headings or as marginalia, appears also to be idiosyncratic (the *ornatus* of Chepe and that of Ludgate are noted marginally [next to lines 258–60 and 351–53] whereas other places get interlined rubrics [before lines 269 and 317]; one of the unscripted accidents gets a marginal annotation [next to lines 250–52] whereas the other two get rubricated headings [before lines 177 and 183]), and it may have been determined by considerations of layout peculiar to this manuscript. The two-columned layout — an important economy for the kind of large collection that the Bodleian manuscript once was — makes marginalia difficult to emplace in outer margins, in the very narrow margins at the gutter by the book's spine, or between the columns mid page. Marginalia do not occur in such positions, where there was no room for them. Therefore, the matter treated in the surviving Bodleian manuscript copy as headings may well all once have been marginalia that migrated into interlinear position when there was no marginal room for them. All this suggests that, though the marginalia and headings may yet be authorial in the sense that Maidstone may have written them (or some of them) himself, they are still late, added after the original composition of the poem, calculated to fit it out for circulation amongst a different readership — not actors of the 1392 crisis, but a more distant (clerical, possibly specifically Carmelite) readership that someone like Richard Lavenham might represent.

Consequently, the present edition relegates the headings and marginalia to the textual apparatus (where they are nevertheless reported in full). Instead, the edited text is divided by line spaces into a series of unheaded sections corresponding to the major divisions in the sequence of events, which are in fact usually given a heading or marginal note in the manuscript. The same reasoning ought to lead also to relegation of the opening lines 1–14 similarly to the apparatus. These lines are a separate item bibliographically: optional, belated, and probably having a different publication or circulation history from lines 15–546, though that history cannot now be recovered. Although 1–14 are not part of the *Concordia* proper, their removal might have confusing practical or other consequences, so they have been kept in the place the manuscript allots them, separated from the rest by line space.

Though the surviving text is somewhat late, it is not greatly so, and the transmission of Maidstone's poem is still not so complex as to have engendered textual confusion. Twice, pentameter lines at least appear to have dropped, and possibly longer passages (after lines 93 and 170), and it may be that the surviving text has other *lacunae* elsewhere that have gone unnoticed. But no obvious transpositions of lines or couplets would appear to have occurred, nor any garbling within lines.[94] For the rest, there are only a handful of readings that want correction, and only correction of simple mechanical errors (see the textual apparatus at lines 79, 177, 345, 364, 407, 442, 467, and 471). All such places, where the edited text departs from the manuscript text, are enclosed in brackets [ ], excepting the marks of punctuation, which are editorial, and the expansion of manuscript abbreviations, which are supplied silently throughout the text. The textual apparatus also gives substantive variants from the editions of Thomas Wright, both of 1838 and of 1859, and Charles Roger Smith, of 1972. At line 330, Smith has what appears to be a conjecture, though no explanation is essayed, and Wright's doings are inevitably of interest. He worked quickly — carelessly even, sometimes — and his variant readings in this poem are always transcription errors, errors in the sense that they are not manuscript readings; on the other hand, Wright transcribed so much contemporary Latin poetry that his transcriptional errors occasionally have the quality of conjectures by effect, possibly reflecting a not fully conscious sense on Wright's part of what his author ought to have written, and so possibly yielding guidance to what his author might have written or did write.

A possible advantage of the editorial decisions taken here about representation of the text — admittedly polemic, intended not to be right so much as to enjoin critical thinking about the text — is that, at the expense of the historical occasion, they highlight the work of the poet, which is stylistically significant. The *Concordia* is written in unrhymed elegiac distychs, and the text is plain in other ways as well, in ways indicative of an intention to open up the subject matter of the poem for a comparatively broad audience. The rhetorical import of the poem's style is anti-hermetic, in other words, meaning not to impress the (clerical, scholastic) few by means of the kind of ornamental hyper-sophistication that can characterize late-medieval Anglo-Latin poetry, but to sway the audience to its propagandistic point of view by plain speaking.

The plain style that Maidstone used, for what remains a formal poem, fundamentally panegyric and official-apologetic, written for an occasion of state, is also a classicizing style in palpable ways, extending from broad structural features of the poem, like the already mentioned emphasis on the oratory of the pageantry's participants, to particulars of versification and syntax, descriptive vocabulary, and patterns of allusion. The classicizing is hardly thoroughgoing or exclusive, nor does it extend to use of the kind of Grecisms, say, or references to antique arcana that can make classicism another hermetic style, performed for the appreciation of the specializedly learned.[95] Still, the classicizing of Maidstone's poem amounts to an acknowledgment on his part that, for performing formal public poetry, the ancient models (of which he shows his awareness) provided useful stylistic guidance.

---

[94] But see lines 93 and 325–26 and the corresponding explanatory notes.

[95] See David R. Carlson, "Whetehamstede on Lollardy: Latin Styles and the Vernacular Cultures of Early Fifteenth-Century England," pp. 37–38.

In fact, Maidstone's versification has the features that distinguish medieval quantitative Latin poetry:[96] regularly, there is lengthening before the strong caesura, in both hexameter and pentameter lines (see Appendix 4.1); and there is shortening of certain word-final vowels that were treated as long in classical Latin verse: final *-o* is consistently short (Appendix 4.2), as is also the final *-e* of adverbs (Appendix 4.3): Maidstone treated as short the final *-e* of such words as *valde, intime, publice*, etc., perhaps by analogy with the commonest adverbs and adverbials, like *bene* or *inde*, or *forte* or *sponte*, having a short final *-e* already in ancient practice. Inconsistencies occur, too, though these are few and minor: three instances where *e* deriving etymologically from the classical Latin diphthong *ae* is treated as short, though in the rather larger majority of cases this kind of vowel remains long (Appendix 4.4); and a similarly circumscribed number of cases, four, where a word-initial *h-* appears to have been treated as a consonant, closing and lengthening a preceding word-final syllable (e.g., line 28 *nēc habet*), though again these four are to be set against the tens or dozens of places in the poem where such an *h-* does not effect this unusual closing (Appendix 4.5). The form *ī nultus* occurs once (line 30) but then later appears *ĭnultus* (line 414); *nĭmis* occurs five times (lines 111, 137, 198, 206, 380) though there is also one *nī mis* (line 209); but with these two exceptions, the quantities of the words in Maidstone's lexicon are internally consistent. Little matter, then, that his regularities are not always classical: in fact, there are more than four dozen remaining instances where Maidstone's quantities do not match classical norms (Appendix 4.6). The sample is not long enough for most of these terms to recur, so it may be that some of these quantities are false (like the anomalous *nī mis*) rather than regularities, albeit unclassical ones; still, when these terms do recur, Maidstone treats them consistently: *ŏdio* in various forms (lines 26, 146, 416), *trōnus* in various forms (lines 319, 459, 495; from CL *thrŏnus*), and oblique cases of *plebs* with a persistently short stem-vowel (lines 426, 489, 532). As in these instances, the majority of Maidstone's "false" quantities involve stem-vowels, where he would have had little or no lexicographic guidance to classical norms. Getting such quantities "right" in his own practice might have been possible by closer application to the study of ancient verse. But Maidstone's prosody ought not to be measured against any putative classical ideal. Ancient norms are not pertinent. Maidstone's prosody is sufficiently consistent internally to be recognizably good quantitative Latin poetry, painstaking even (Maidstone avoids elision, for example, all but completely: the single instance is "senatorio, urbs" [line 73]); moreover, the standard Maidstone's verse achieves is not idiosyncratic but was sanctioned by the contemporary practice of other Latin poets.

---

[96] For these, see A. G. Rigg, "Metrics," in *Medieval Latin: An Introduction and Bibliographical Guide*, ed. F. A. C. Mantello and A. G. Rigg (Washington, DC: Catholic University of America Press, 1996), pp. 106–10, and the appendix "Metre," in *A History of Anglo-Latin Literature*, especially pp. 313–14. There is analysis of Maidstone's prosody in Smith, "*Concordia*," pp. 113–21.

Though for the most part Maidstone avoids it, there is still a little rhyme. There are three properly disyllable-rhymed leonine lines ("Quales texture picturarumque figure" [line 265], for example; also lines 182 and 397). Mostly, however, Maidstone's rhymes involve only single syllables ("Pinxerat hic celum arte iuvante novum" [line 62], for example; also lines 63, 75, 181, 238, 272), of a sort that could hardly be avoided and is hardly noticeable. The exception may be the poem's final six lines, each of which has single-syllable rhyme of strong caesura with line-ending (though "Sint sibi felices anni mensesque diesque" [line 543] squints), yielding perhaps a heightened sense of imminent conclusion. However, there is none of the ostentatious couplet rhyming that characterizes more mannered Latin verse, of line-endings nor of consecutive caesuras (but see lines 181–82), nor of cross-rhyming caesuras and line-endings. Alliteration is restricted to the closing couplet of the detachable verse exordium (lines 13–14) and to the passage describing the brief storm (lines 177–80), where occurs the sequence *Tunc - tristis - Tempestas - turbinis - tristis - tunc - Turbari - turbine - tam valido*.

The middle or plain way that this treatment of rhyme represents — not much, one way or the other, but nothing exclusive — is characteristic of Maidstone's style generally. He is capable of an egregious mannerism like "Westquemonasterium" (line 454), yielding a four-word pentameter, fully half of which is given over to this one term, with the properly enclitic *-que* embedded in it; nevertheless, there is but the one example. Also, there are instances of paranomasiastic wordplay — "Quis numerare queat numerum turbe numerose" (line 67), for example; likewise "Sicque pium miseri miseret solitum misereri" (line 189) and "Femina feminea sua dum sic femina nudat" (line 251) — but even these lines are not hard, and three of them in over five hundred lines represents restraint.[97] Syntactically, too, Maidstone's work is plain: for the most part, he favors simple declarative statements, simple compounding sentences, consecutive clause arrangement (rather than embedding), and prosaic word orders, without taxing hyperbaton. The preponderantly dactylic rhythms of Maidstone's lines (Appendix 4.7) probably also contribute to the impression of lightness or conversational ease about the verse, by contrast with the more ponderous, incantory effects that heavily spondaic lines can yield.[98]

---

[97] See also the repetition *Salve - salve - Salvet - salus* in the line-initial and line-final positions of lines 393–94.

[98] When Maidstone does use heavily spondaic lines, they can be strikingly effective: e.g., line 257 "Spectantur pulcre, dum spectant ista, puelle" (see also lines 134 and 232). Line-initial pairs or strings of monosyllabic words (e.g., line 477 "Hinc, mi rex, mi dulcis amor") are rare herein, too — there are only 24 instances in 546 lines (4.4%) — and Maidstone's avoidance of first-foot spondees — an ancient and widespread avoidance, though reversible in some schools (see Andy Orchard, "After Aldhelm: The Teaching and Transmission of the Anglo-Latin Hexameter," pp. 100–03 and 107–08) — is general: only 93 instances (17.0%). Maidstone's lines still less frequently end with monosyllables, singly or in pairs (never more than pairs): there are only 12 instances in the whole poem (2.2%), remarkably nine of them

The vocabulary admits various English-derived or otherwise contemporary terms, of a sort that would or could not have occurred in Republican or Augustan writers. The terms occur thickly where Maidstone describes or mentions contemporary institutions and practices; for example, in the passages describing the *mysterii* ("guilds") arrayed to welcome King Richard (lines 79–95). The passage listing the guilds also contains most of the somewhat *recherché* Grecisms Maidstone resorts to: *apothecarius* (line 83), *zonarius* (line 89), *pandoxator* (line 91), and *cirotecarius* (line 94), for example.[99] These are not numerous, and Maidstone uses Latinized English words here too, like *carpentarius* (line 85) and *candelarius* (line 90). When dealing even with contemporary institutions and practices, however, Maidstone favors classicizing references: the London aldermen — Maidstone does use *aldirmannos* (line 72) — are represented as a *senatus* (line 73), going about London — usually called New Troy (lines 11, 17, 39, and 123, though compare 20 and 148)[100] — *toga*-clad (lines 76, 132, 165); and King Richard finally addresses the assembled *senatus populusque* of the city from a *tribunal* (line 461). Phoebus appears (line 17) in the middle of a passage in which a date is given medieval-style (lines 15–19), rather than in terms of calends and ides; on the other hand, Maidstone gives a distance in *stadia* (line 101), though evidently he uses the term to mean "paces," and the direction of the wind is given, not in compass-points, but in poetic Roman terms: *Nothus* and *Favonius* (line 181).

Likewise, the allusions in the poem tend to be more literary than scriptural, and the literary ones tend to be classical, though they are not exclusively so. The only biblical references not imposed on Maidstone by the pageantry itself (e.g., John the Baptist's ejaculation "Agnus et ecce dei" [line 372], confirmed by the other sources) are the likenings of Queen Anne to Esther (line 441)[101] and of King Richard once to Solomon (line 38) and again later to Absolon (line 112). Maidstone mentions St. Erkenwald (line 348), to whose shrine the procession took the king, and in honor of whose cult a surviving Middle English poem had just been or was just

---

at the end of pentameter lines. Maidstone's line-endings in his pentameters are very variable and informal, however, where 12.1% (33 of 272 pentameter lines) end, unclassically, with terms of other than two or three syllables (and the number of trisyllable pentameter endings is high for post-Ovidian verse: here 42 of 272 pentameters [15.4%]).

[99] Other Grecisms in the poem include: *phalanga* (line 100), *phalera* (line 236), *dyademata* (line 299), and *ierarchia* (line 330).

[100] On these Trojan allusions in Maidstone, see Federico, "A Fourteenth-Century Erotics of Politics," pp. 121–29 and 152–53. Some background is discussed in John Clark, "Trinovantum — The Evolution of a Legend," pp. 146–48.

[101] On this allusion, see Strohm, "Queens as Intercessors," pp. 110 and 96–98.

about to be written;[102] unprompted by events, Maidstone also likens King Richard to Troilus (line 112), lately lent prominence by the single major poem Chaucer actually finished, c. 1385, and made public. King Arthur's name comes up, along with that of his Trojan forebear Brutus (lines 479–80); for the most part, however, the references are to antiquities: Amazons, Phaeton, Venus, and Mars put in appearances (lines 123, 250, 117, and 98 respectively); King Richard comes to the city also like a Paris (line 26) and a Caesar (line 200); Tethys is away, and instead the city's conduits run with Bacchus (line 269). The surviving introductory lines quote Cicero by name (lines 1–6) — a figure evidently of special interest to Lavenham — and the one embedded quotation in the poem I find is from Ovid (line 293).

To have made King Richard a Caesar come again, like making the civic delegation that greeted him a senate, was to magnify. Maidstone's classicism generally had this as one of its effects: it served to decorate and so to honor the occasion, as did also his decision to write verse, as did also his decision to write at all. However taken, by authorial initiative or by official commission, this decision had a double consequence, legible in the poem: it enjoined glorifying the monarch and also reaching out to a public. The classicizing plain style served both ends. Maidstone's *Concordia* shows Anglo-Latin poetry, on a specific occasion, in the process of making itself a public poetry — a broadly appealing, flexible, legible medium for addressing public issues.[103]

---

[102] Clifford Peterson, *Saint Erkenwald*, pp. 11–14, discusses the evidence suggesting that the same bishop of London who figures in Maidstone's *Concordia* (line 345) would have had something to contribute to creation of the circumstances in which the Middle English poem was composed. Like Maidstone, Braybroke was an anti-Lollard activist and, concomitantly, a promoter of orthodoxies, like the cult of the saints, as a bulwark against deviance; Gordon Whatley, "Heathens and Saints: *St. Erkenwald* in Its Legendary Context," pp. 353–63, emphasizes the poem's doctrinal conservatism. In the years just before 1392, Braybroke was responsible for elevation of the cult of St. Erkenwald — a legendary figure for having built a strong, dogmatically righteous church in London at an earlier time of heterodoxy, including persistent paganism — and the 1392 procession's visit to the shrine of St. Erkenwald in St. Paul's, featured in Maidstone's poem (lines 343–48) though in none of the other sources, ought to be regarded as part of Braybroke's promotional campaign. On the circumstances of the *Erkenwald*'s composition, see Frank Grady, "*St. Erkenwald* and the Merciless Parliament."

[103] This process is described by Rigg, "Anglo-Latin in the Ricardian Age," pp. 129–32. The fundamental discussion remains that of Anne Middleton, "The Idea of Public Poetry in the Reign of Richard II," though Middleton omits to consider Latin-language evidence.

Select Bibliography

Bale, John. *Index Britanniae Scriptorum*. Ed. Caroline Brett and James Carley. Cambridge, UK: D. S. Brewer, 1990.

Barron, Caroline M. "The Tyranny of Richard II." *Bulletin of the Institute of Historical Research* 41 (1968), 1–18.

——. "The Quarrel of Richard II with London 1392–7." In *The Reign of Richard II: Essays in Honour of May McKisack*. Ed. F. R. H. Du Boulay and Caroline M. Barron. London: Athlone Press, 1971. Pp. 173–201.

Bennett, J. A. W. *Chaucer at Oxford and at Cambridge*. Toronto: University of Toronto Press, 1974.

Bird, Ruth. *The Turbulent London of Richard II*. Intro. James Tait. London: Longmans, Green and Co., 1949.

Blanchard, W. Scott. "The Negative Dialectic of Lorenzo Valla: A Study in the Pathology of Opposition." *Renaissance Studies* 14 (2000), 149–89.

Bokenham, Osbern. *Legendys of Hooly Wommen*. Ed. Mary S. Serjeantson. EETS o.s. 206. London: Oxford University Press, 1938.

Bowers, John M. "*Pearl* in Its Royal Setting: Ricardian Poetry Revisited." *Studies in the Age of Chaucer* 17 (1995), 111–55.

Boyle, Leonard E. "The *Oculus Sacerdotis* and Some Other Works of William of Pagula." *Transactions of the Royal Historical Society* fifth ser. 5 (1955), 81–110.

Broughton, Bradford B. *The Legends of King Richard I, Coeur de Lion: A Study of Sources and Variations to the Year 1600*. The Hague: Mouton, 1966.

Carlson, David R. "The Civic Poetry of Abbot John Whethamstede of St. Albans († 1465)." *Mediaeval Studies* 61 (1999), 205–42.

——. "Whetehamstede on Lollardy: Latin Styles and the Vernacular Cultures of Early Fifteenth-Century England." *Journal of English and Germanic Philology* 102 (2003), 21–41.

Catto, Jeremy I. "Wyclif and Wycliffism at Oxford 1356–1430." In *History of the University of Oxford.* Volume II: *Late Medieval Oxford.* Ed. J. I. Catto and Ralph Evans. Oxford: Clarendon Press, 1992. Pp. 175–261.

Chrimes, S. B. *English Constitutional Ideas in the Fifteenth Century.* Cambridge, UK: The University Press, 1936.

Clark, John. "Trinovantum — The Evolution of a Legend." *Journal of Medieval History* 7 (1981), 135–51.

Clopper, Lawrence M. "The Engaged Spectator: Langland and Chaucer on Civic Spectacle and the *Theatrum.*" *Studies in the Age of Chaucer* 22 (2000), 115–39.

Condren, Edward I. "The Historical Context of the *Book of the Duchess*: A New Hypothesis." *Chaucer Review* 5 (1971), 195–212.

Crompton, James. "*Fasciculi Zizaniorum.*" *Journal of Ecclesiastical History* 12 (1961), 35–45 and 155–66.

Curtius, Ernst Robert. *European Literature and the Latin Middle Ages.* Trans. Willard R. Trask. Bollingen Series 36. 1953; rpt. Princeton: Princeton University Press, 1973.

Dahmus, Joseph H. *The Prosecution of John Wyclyf.* New Haven: Yale University Press, 1952; rpt. Hamden, CT: Archon Press, 1970.

Day, Mabel, ed. *The Wheatley Manuscript, a Collection of Middle English Verse and Prose Contained in a MS, Now in the British Museum, Add. Mss. 39574.* EETS o.s. 155. London: Oxford University Press, 1921.

Duckworth, George E. *Vergil and Classical Hexameter Poetry: A Study in Metrical Variety.* Ann Arbor: University of Michigan Press, 1969.

Duffy, Eamon. *The Stripping of the Altars: Traditional Religion in England c.1400–c.1580.* New Haven: Yale University Press, 1992.

Dymmok, Roger. *Liber contra xii errores et hereses lollardorum.* Ed. H. S. Cronin. Wyclif Society. London: K. Paul, Trench, Trübner and Co., Ltd., 1922.

Eberle, Patricia J. "The Politics of Courtly Style at the Court of Richard II." In *The Spirit of the Court*. Ed. Glyn S. Burgess and Robert A. Taylor. Cambridge, UK: D. S. Brewer, 1985. Pp. 168–78.

Edden, Valerie. "Richard Maidstone's *Penitential Psalms*." *Leeds Studies in English* n.s. 17 (1986), 77–94.

———. "The Debate between Richard Maidstone and the Lollard Ashwardby (ca. 1390)." *Carmelus* 34 (1987), 113–34.

———, ed. *Richard Maidstone's Penitential Psalms*. Middle English Texts 22. Heidelberg: C. Winter Universitätsverlag, 1990.

Eisner, Sigmund, ed. *The Kalendarium of Nicholas of Lynn*. Trans. Gary Mac Eoin and Sigmund Eisner. The Chaucer Library. Athens: University of Georgia Press, 1980.

Emden, Alfred Brotherston. *A Biographical Register of the University of Oxford to A. D. 1500*. 3 vols. Oxford: Clarendon Press, 1957–59.

Federico, Sylvia. "A Fourteenth-Century Erotics of Politics: London as a Feminine New Troy." *Studies in the Age of Chaucer* 19 (1997), 121–55.

Forde, Simon. "Nicholas Hereford's Ascension Day Sermon, 1382." *Mediaeval Studies* 51 (1989), 205–41.

Galbraith, V. H., ed. *The Anonimalle Chronicle 1333 to 1381*. Manchester: Manchester University Press, 1927; rpt. 1970.

Galloway, Andrew. "The Literature of 1388 and the Politics of Pity in Gower's *Confessio amantis*." In *The Letter of the Law: Legal Practice and Literary Production in Medieval England*. Ed. Emily Steiner and Candace Barrington. Ithaca: Cornell University Press, 2002. Pp. 67–104.

Geoffrey of Monmouth. *The History of the Kings of Britain*. Trans. Lewis Thorpe. Harmondsworth: Penguin, 1966.

Gillespie, Vincent. "*Doctrina* and *Predicacio*: The Design and Function of Some Pastoral Manuals." *Leeds Studies in English* n.s. 11 (1980), 36–50.

Given-Wilson, Chris. "Wealth and Credit, Public and Private: The Earls of Arundel 1306–1397." *English Historical Review* 106 (1991), 1–26.

——. "Adam Usk, the Monk of Evesham and the Parliament of 1397–8." *Historical Research* 66 (1993), 329–35.

——. "The Manner of King Richard's Renunciation: A 'Lancastrian Narrative'?" *English Historical Review* 108 (1993), 365–70.

——, ed. and trans. *Chronicles of the Revolution 1397–1400: The Reign of Richard II*. Manchester: Manchester University Press, 1993.

Goodman, Anthony. *John of Gaunt: The Exercise of Princely Power in Fourteenth-Century Europe*. London: Longman, 1992.

Grady, Frank. "*St. Erkenwald* and the Merciless Parliament." *Studies in the Age of Chaucer* 22 (2000), 179–211.

Gransden, Antonia. "Propaganda in English Medieval Historiography." *Journal of Medieval History* 1 (1975), 363–81.

Hammond, Eleanor Prescott. *Chaucer: A Bibliographical Manual*. 1908; rpt. New York: Peter Smith, 1933.

Hanrahan, Michael. "'A Straunge Succesour Sholde Take Youre Heritage': The *Clerk's Tale* and the Crisis of Ricardian Rule." *Chaucer Review* 35 (2001), 335–50.

Hector, L. C., and Barbara F. Harvey, eds. and trans. *The Westminster Chronicle 1381–1394*. Oxford: Clarendon Press, 1982.

Hoccleve, Thomas. *The Regiment of Princes*. Ed. Charles R. Blyth. Kalamazoo, MI: Medieval Institute Publications, 1999.

Holmes, George. *The Good Parliament*. Oxford: Clarendon Press, 1975.

Hudson, Anne. *Selections from English Wycliffite Writings*. Cambridge: Cambridge University Press, 1978; rpt. Toronto: University of Toronto Press, 1997.

——. "A New Look at the Lay Folks' Catechism." *Viator* 16 (1985), 243–58.

Hudson, Anne. *The Premature Reformation: Wycliffite Texts and Lollard History.* Oxford: Clarendon Press, 1988.

James, Mervyn. "English Politics and the Concept of Honour, 1485–1642." *Past and Present* Supplement 3. Oxford: Past and Present Society, 1978. Rpt. in *Society, Politics and Culture: Studies in Early Modern England.* Cambridge, UK: Cambridge University Press, 1986. Pp. 308–415.

Justice, Steven. *Writing and Rebellion: England in 1381.* Berkeley: University of California Press, 1994.

Kipling, Gordon. "Triumphal Drama: Form in English Civic Pageantry." *Renaissance Drama* n.s. 8 (1977), 37–56.

——. "The London Pageants for Margaret of Anjou: A Medieval Script Restored." *Medieval English Theatre* 4 (1982), 5–27.

——. "Richard II's 'Sumptuous Pageants' and the Idea of the Civic Triumph." In *Pageantry in the Shakespearean Theater.* Ed. David M. Bergeron. Athens: University of Georgia Press, 1985. Pp. 83–103.

Kreuzer, James R. "Richard Maidstone's Version of the Fifty-First Psalm." *Modern Language Notes* 66 (1951), 224–31.

Latham, R. E. *Revised Medieval Latin Word-List from British and Irish Sources.* London: British Academy, 1965.

Lewis, N. B. "The Anniversary Service for Blanche, Duchess of Lancaster, 12th September, 1374." *Bulletin of the John Rylands Library* 21 (1937), 176–92.

Lindenbaum, Sheila. "The Smithfield Tournament of 1390." *Journal of Medieval and Renaissance Studies* 20 (1990), 1–20.

Loach, Jennifer. "The Function of Ceremonial in the Reign of Henry VIII." *Past & Present* 142 (1994), 43–68.

Mantello, F. A. C., and A. G. Rigg, eds. *Medieval Latin: An Introduction and Bibliographical Guide.* Washington, DC: Catholic University of America Press, 1996.

Martin, G. H., ed. and trans. *Knighton's Chronicle 1337–1396*. Oxford: Clarendon Press, 1995.

Matheson, Lister M. *The Prose Brut: The Development of a Middle English Chronicle*. Tempe, AZ: Medieval & Renaissance Texts & Studies, 1998.

Mathew, Gervase. *The Court of Richard II*. London: Murray, 1968.

Middleton, Anne. "The Idea of Public Poetry in the Reign of Richard II." *Speculum* 53 (1978), 94–114.

Nightingale, Pamela. "Capitalists, Crafts and Constitutional Change in Late Fourteenth-Century London." *Past & Present* 124 (1989), 3–35.

———. "The Growth of London in the Medieval English Economy." In *Progress and Problems in Medieval England: Essays in Honour of Edward Miller*. Ed. Richard Britnell and John Hatcher. Cambridge, UK: Cambridge University Press, 1996. Pp. 89–106.

———. "Knights and Merchants: Trade, Politics and the Gentry in Late Medieval England." *Past & Present* 169 (2000), 36–62.

Orchard, Andy. "After Aldhelm: The Teaching and Transmission of the Anglo-Latin Hexameter." *Journal of Medieval Latin* 2 (1992), 96–133.

Palmer, J[ohn] J. N. "The Historical Context of the *Book of the Duchess*: A Revision." *Chaucer Review* 8 (1974), 253–61.

———. "Froissart et le Héraut Chandos." *Le moyen âge* 88 (1982), 271–92.

Paris, Gaston. "Le roman de Richard Coeur de Lion." *Romania* 26 (1897), 353–93.

Parker, Roscoe E., ed. *The Middle English Stanzaic Versions of the Life of Saint Anne*. EETS o.s. 174. London: Oxford University Press, 1928.

Patterson, Lee W. "The 'Parson's Tale' and the Quitting of the 'Canterbury Tales.'" *Traditio* 34 (1978), 331–80.

Pearsall, Derek. *The Life of Geoffrey Chaucer: A Critical Biography*. Oxford: Blackwell, 1992.

Peterson, Clifford, ed. *Saint Erkenwald*. Philadelphia: University of Pennsylvania Press, 1977.

Pfander, H. G. "Some Medieval Manuals of Religious Instruction in England and Observations on Chaucer's Parson's Tale." *Journal of English and Germanic Philology* 35 (1936), 243–58.

Platnauer, Maurice. *Latin Elegiac Verse: A Study of the Metrical Usages of Tibullus, Propertius & Ovid*. Cambridge, UK: Cambridge University Press, 1951.

Power, Eileen. *The Wool Trade in English Medieval History, Being the Ford Lectures*. London: Oxford University Press, 1941.

Rigg, A. G. *A History of Anglo-Latin Literature, 1066–1422*. Cambridge, UK: Cambridge University Press, 1992.

——. "Anglo-Latin in the Ricardian Age." In *Essays on Ricardian Literature in Honour of J. A. Burrow*. Ed. A. J. Minnis, Charlotte C. Morse, and Thorlac Turville-Petre. Oxford: Clarendon Press, 1997. Pp. 121–41.

Russell, G. H. "Vernacular Instruction of the Laity in the Later Middle Ages in England: Some Texts and Notes." *Journal of Religious History* 2 (1962), 98–119.

Saul, Nigel. "Richard II and the Vocabulary of Kingship." *English Historical Review* 110 (1995), 854–77.

——. *Richard II*. New Haven: Yale University Press, 1997.

Sayles, George Osborne. "King Richard II of England: A Fresh Look." *Proceedings of the American Philosophical Society* 115 (1971), 28–31.

——. "The Deposition of Richard II: Three Lancastrian Narratives." *Bulletin of the Institute of Historical Research* 54 (1981), 257–70.

Smith, Charles Roger. "*Concordia: Facta inter Regem Riccardum II et civitatem Londonie per Fratrum Riccardum Maydiston, Carmelitam, Sacre Theologie Doctorem, Anno Domine 1393*, Edited with Introduction, Translation, and Notes." Ph.D. Diss., Princeton University, 1972.

Somerset, Fiona. "Answering the *Twelve Conclusions*: Dymmok's Halfhearted Gestures towards Publication." In *Lollardy and the Gentry in the Later Middle Ages*. Ed. Margaret Aston and Colin Richmond. New York: St. Martin's Press, 1997. Pp. 52–76.

Somerset, Fiona. *Clerical Discourse and Lay Audience in Late Medieval England*. Cambridge, UK: Cambridge University Press, 1998.

Spade, Paul Vincent. "The Treatises *On Modal Propositions* and *On Hypothetical Propositions* by Richard Lavenham." *Mediaeval Studies* 35 (1973), 49–59.

Staley, Lynn. "Gower, Richard II, Henry of Derby, and the Business of Making Culture." *Speculum* 75 (2000), 68–96.

Strachey, John, ed. *Rotuli parliamentorum; ut et petitiones, et placita in parliamento*. Comp. Richard Blyke et al. 6 vols. London: [s. n.], 1767–77.

Strohm, Paul. *Hochon's Arrow: The Social Imagination of Fourteenth-Century Texts*. Princeton: Princeton University Press, 1992. [See especially ch. 3, "The Textual Environment of Chaucer's 'Lak of Stedfastnesse,'" pp. 55–74; ch. 5, "Queens as Intercessors," pp. 95–119; and appendix 2, "The Literature of Livery," pp. 179–85.]

——. "Trade, Treason, and the Murder of Janus Imperial." *Journal of British Studies* 35 (1996), 1–23.

Suggett, Helen. "A Letter Describing Richard II's Reconciliation with the City of London, 1392." *English Historical Review* 62 (1947), 209–13.

Taylor, Andrew. "Anne of Bohemia and the Making of Chaucer." *Studies in the Age of Chaucer* 19 (1997), 95–119.

Taylor, John. "Richard II's Views on Kingship." *Proceedings of the Leeds Philosophical and Literary Society, Literary and Historical Section* 14 (1971), 189–205.

Tentler, Thomas N. "The *Summa* for Confessors as an Instrument of Social Control." In *The Pursuit of Holiness in Late Medieval and Renaissance Religion*. Ed. Charles Trinkaus and Heiko A. Oberman. Leiden: E. J. Brill, 1974. Pp. 103–26. [See also responses by Leonard E. Boyle and William J. Bouwsma, with reply by Tentler, pp. 126–37.]

——. *Sin and Confession on the Eve of the Reformation*. Princeton: Princeton University Press, 1977.

Thompson, John J. "Literary Associations of an Anonymous Middle English Paraphrase of Vulgate Psalm L." *Medium Aevum* 57 (1988), 38–55.

Thrupp, Sylvia L. "Social Control in the Medieval Town." *Journal of Economic History* 1 Supplement (1941), 39–52.

Tout, T. F. *Chapters in the Administrative History of Mediaeval England: The Wardrobe, the Chamber and the Small Seals*. 6 vols. Manchester: Manchester University Press, 1920–33; rpt. 1967.

Unwin, George. *The Gilds and Companies of London*. Third ed. London: G. Allen & Unwin, 1938.

Wallace, David. *Chaucerian Polity: Absolutist Lineages and Associational Forms in England and Italy*. Stanford: Stanford University Press, 1997.

Warner of Rouen. *Moriuht: Warner of Rouen, a Norman Latin Poem from the Early Eleventh Century*. Ed. Christopher J. McDonough. Studies and Texts 121. Toronto: Pontifical Institute of Mediaeval Studies, 1995.

Whatley, Gordon. "Heathens and Saints: *St. Erkenwald* in Its Legendary Context." *Speculum* 61 (1986), 330–63.

Whittingham, Selby. "The Chronology of the Portraits of Richard II." *Burlington Magazine* 113 (1971), 12–21.

Wickert, Maria. *Studien zu John Gower*. Cologne: Kölner Universitäts-Verlag, 1953.

Wickham, Glynne. *Early English Stages 1300 to 1660*. 3 vols. Second ed. London: Routledge and Kegan Paul, 1980.

Williams, Arnold. "*Protectorium Pauperis*, a Defense of the Begging Friars by Richard Maidstone, O. Carm. (d. 1396)." *Carmelus* 5 (1958), 132–80.

Williams, Gwyn A. *Medieval London: From Commune to Capital*. London: Athlone Press, 1963.

Wright, Thomas, ed. *Alliterative Poem on the Deposition of King Richard II: Ricardi Maydiston de concordia inter Richard II et civitatem London*. Camden Society [First Series] 3. London: J. B. Nichols and Son, 1838; rpt. New York: Johnson Reprint Corp., 1968.

Introduction

Wright, Thomas. *Political Poems and Songs Relating to English History Composed during the Period from the Accession of Edw. III. to That of Ric. III*. Rolls Series 14. 2 vols. London: Longman, Green, Longman, and Roberts, 1859–61.

Concordia facta inter regem et cives Londonie, per fratrem Riccardum Maydiston

TULLIUS IN laudem tantam sustollit amicos [*fol. 8vb*]
    Quod licet, hiis demptis, optima nil valeant.
"Stes," ait, "in celis, videas ibi queque beata,
    Hauriat auris in hiis utraque dulce melos:
5   Quicquid adhuc sensus poterit tibi pascere quinos
    Nil valet acceptum, si nec amicus adest.
Si careas socio, cui sata placencia narres,
    Hec eadem sentis non placuisse tibi."
Hinc tibi, Ricarde, duplante iugo michi iuncte
10   (Nomen et omen habes: sic socius meus es),
Gaudia visa michi Trenovantum nuper in urbe
    Actus amicicia glisco referre modo;
Et licet incultum carmen tibi condere curem,
    Parce, precor, cure: parcere debet amor.

15   M CAPE, TER quoque C, deciesque novem duo iunge
    (Hunc numerum anni supputo dando notis).
Tunc bis ter Phebo fuerat soror associata,
    Cum bona felici sunt, Nova Troia, tibi.
Mensis ut Augusti ter septima fulsit in orbem
20   Lux, tibi, Londonie, rumor amenus adest;
Namque tuum regem, sponsum dominumque tuumque,
    Quem tibi sustulerat Perfida Lingua, capis.
Invidiosa cohors regem tibi vertit in iram,
    Desereret thalamum sponsus ut ipse suum;
25   Sed quia totus amor tuus est — et amantis ymago
    Formosior Paride — nescit odisse diu.
Adde quod in miseros semper solet hic misereri,
    Nec habet ultrices rex pius iste manus.
Quot mala, quot mortes tenero sit passus ab evo,
30   Quamque sit inultus, Anglia tota videt.
Quid cupit hic servire deo, nisi semper et esse

The Reconciliation of Richard II with London, by Brother Richard Maidstone

In praise of friends does Tully lavish such great praise,
    For, with those gone, the best of things, though good, lack worth.
"In heaven you might stand and see where all is blest
    And with both ears there drink in that sweet song," he says,
5   "But all that nourishes our fivefold wits and sense
    Is not a bit of good without a friend beside.
If you're without a soul to share your pleasure with,
    You feel that none of this has brought you any joy."
So, Richard, who are joined to me by double yoke
10   (You share my name and symbol: we're companions),
To you I'm drawn by friendship, and I long to tell
    The joys I saw just recently at Trinovant;
I hesitate to offer you a clumsy song:
    Have pity on my fear, I beg, as love demands.

15   TAKE M, THREE C's, and ten times nine, and then add two
    (I calculate the number of the year by signs).
Six times the moon had to her twin, the sun, been joined,
    When happy tidings came to you, O glad New Troy.
When three times seven August dawns had lit the world,
20   A pleasant rumor, London, spread throughout your bounds;
For now you get your king again, your spouse, your lord,
    Whom Wicked Tongue had taken from you by deceit.
Its grudging troop had roused the king to wrath at you,
    So that the groom gave up and left his marriage bed;
25   But since your love is whole — your lover's face more fair
    Than even that of Paris — he can't hate for long.
And one thing more: this gentle king commiserates
    With those that grieve — his hands are not avenger's hands.
All England sees how many ills, how many deaths,
30   He's suffered from a tender age, still unavenged.
What service will he offer God? He'll always be

Pacificum, letum, nilque perire bonum?
Sic fovet ecclesiam, statuens statuum moderamen,
    Sternere ne liceat quod statuere patres.
35   Effugat ingratos, cupidos, stolidos, truculentos:
    Queque decent regem hec rapit ipse sibi.
Talis adolescens toto non restat in orbe,
    Qui sciat ut Salomon regna tenere sua.
Hic licet accensus foret in te, Troia, parumper,
40   Grata modo facies se docet esse piam.
Non poterat mordax detractans lingua tenere
    Quin cuperet thalamum sponsus adire suum.
Qui libertates solitas tibi dempserat omnes
    Nunc redit, et plures reddere promptus eas.
45   Urbis custodem miles quem rex ibi signat
    Alloquitur cives sic, rutilante die:
"Regis in occursum vestri vos este parati,   *[fol. 9ra]*
    Percipiatque palam quam bene nunc veniat.
Tocius ecclesie fiat processio cleri,
50   Omnis et ordo suas se ferat ante cruces.
Nulla sit ars urbis que non distincta seorsum
    Splendidius solito trans vada vadat eques.
Quicquid in urbe probum fuerit promatur in ista
    (Nam gaudete) die: pax tribuetur," ait.
55   Hiis animata loquelis tota cohors sociatur,
    Preparat et cultu se meliore suo;
Ornat et interea se pulcre queque platea:
    Vestibus auratis urbs micat innumeris.
Floris odoriferi specie fragrante platea,
60   Pendula perque domos purpura nulla deest,
Aurea, coccinea, bissinaque tinctaque vestis
    Pinxerat hic celum arte iuvante novum.
Quos tulit ante dies istos plebs ista labores,
    Quas tulit expensas, os reserare nequit.
65   Quid moror? Ecce, dies transit: properatur ab urbe
    Regis in occursum, coniugis atque sue.
Quis numerare queat numerum turbe numerose,
    Que velud astra poli densius inde fluit?
Milia viginti iuvenes numerantur equestres;
70   Qui pedibus pergunt non capit hos numerus.

In peace and joy, and never let the good decline.
He tends the church, decreeing guidance for its ranks
    Not to destroy that which our ancestors decreed.
35 He drives away unruly, greedy, stubborn fools
    And takes unto himself all that befits a king.
In all the world there's no young man alive like him,
    Who knows how, just like Salomon, to rule his realm.
Although his anger, Troy, blazed at you for a while,
40   His face, now pleasing, shows that he is merciful.
Detraction's biting tongue could not detain the king
    From yearning to approach his marriage bed as spouse.
He'd once withdrawn all of your former liberties
    But now returns, quite ready to increase them more.
45 The knight appointed by the king as London's ward
    Addressed the citizens, when dawning day grew red:
"Be now prepared, O Londoners, to meet your king:
    Let him now see how welcome he is to you all.
Let all the clergy of the church proceed in front,
50   And every order bear their crosses held before.
Let every city guild be quite distinct, and then
    On horseback cross the river in a splendid style.
Let all that's good in London be displayed," he said,
    "And on that day rejoice, for then will peace be yours."
55 Emboldened by these words the company drew close,
    And dressed itself in all the best array it could;
Meanwhile, each city square put on its finery:
    The city shone with countless gilden draperies.
The city squares smelled sweet with varied scented blooms,
60   And purple buntings hung throughout in every home,
Cloth stained with gold and white and cocchineal dye
    Had here displayed a canopy with aiding skill.
No tongue could tell the labors or the great expense
    That Londoners had undergone before these days.
65 But look, the day goes by, I mustn't hesitate:
    All rush from town to meet the king and his young bride.
Who could recount the number of that countless crowd
    That flows from London, thicker than the heaven's stars?
On horseback twenty thousand young men could be seen;
70   Of those on foot no number could contain them all.

Custos precedit, comitantur eumque quater sex,
    Quos aldirmannos urbs habet ut proceres.
(Iure senatorio, urbs hiis regitur quasi Roma,
    Hiisque preest maior, quem populus legerit.)
75   Hiis erat ornatus albus color et rubicundus,
    Hos partita toga segregat a reliquis.
Clavibus assumptis, urbis gladio quoque, custos
    Precedit, proceres subque sequntur eum,
H[o]s sequitur phalerata cohors cuiuslibet artis.
80   Secta docet sortem quemque tenere suam:
Hic argentarius, hic piscarius, secus illum
    Mercibus hic deditus, venditor atque meri;
Hic apothecarius, pistor, pictor, lathomusque;
    Hic cultellarius, tonsor, et armifaber;
85   Hic carpentarius, scissor, sartor, ibi sutor;
    Hic pelliparius fulloque, mango, faber;
Hic sunt archifices, ibi carnifices, ibi tector;
    Hic lorimarius pannariusque simul;
[Hic] vaginator, hic zonarius, ibi textor;
90   Hic candelarius, cerarius pariter;
Hic pandoxator, ibi streparius, ibi iunctor;
    Est ibi pomilio, sic avigerulus hic.
"A" super "R" gratis stat in artibus hic numeratis
    [. . . . . . .]
Hic cirotecarius bursistaque, caupo coqusque:
95   Ars patet ex secta singula queque sua.   [*fol. 9rb*]
Cerneret has turmas quisquis puto non dubitaret
    Cernere se formas ordinis angelici.
Tam valido solet auxilio qui Marcius exstat
    Prelia suffultus nulla timere pugil.
100   Quelibet ut proprias est ars sortita phalangas;
    Mille quater stadiis omne repletur iter.

PSALLITE NUNC, cives; regi nunc psallite vestro!
    En, rex vester adest; psallite, quod sapit hic!
Rege propinquante, comites glomerantur heriles.
105   Ha, michi! Quam pulcrum cernere credis eos!
Dum niveo resideret equo, se quique retractant
    Ut pateat populo rex pius ipse suo.

The warden goes before with twenty-four in train,
    For these are London's aldermen, of noble rank.
(Like Rome, the city's ruled by them, as senators,
    And over them the mayor, elected by the folk.)
75   These were arrayed in finery of red and white,
    Distinguished from the rest by robes of double hue.
The warden goes before, the city's keys in hand
    And, too, the city's sword; the nobles walk behind,
Then after this a decked-out troop from every guild.
80   Their suit proclaims that each one is quite separate:
A goldsmith, a fishmonger, and after him
    A mercer bent on trade, a seller of fine wine,
A grocer, baker, painter, and a stonemason,
    A knife-maker, a barber, and an armorer,
85   A carpenter, a shearer, tailor, shoemaker,
    A skinner, dyer, shopmonger, a smith as well,
And here the bowmen, butchers, and the thatchers too,
    The lorimers and drapers too, they came along;
A sheather, girdler, were here, a weaver there,
90   A chandler and a waxmaker were there as well;
A brewer and a stirruper, a joiner too,
    As well there was a fruiterer and poulterer.
Among these guilds a welcome "A" stands on an "R"
    [. . . . . .]
A glover, pursemaker, a taverner, a cook:
95   From each one's suit of clothes, his craft was clear to see.
No one, I think, who saw these crowds, could hesitate
    To say that here he saw the forms of angels stand.
On such support the martial warrior relies
    When he goes forth to war and fears no battle fray.
100   There each and every guild was granted its own troop;
    The route was packed along the way for four full miles.

NOW SING, O citizens, now sing to greet your king!
    For, see, your king is here; now sing, for he is wise!
The king draws near; the noble companies pack close.
105   O my! How fair a sight, you'll grant, to see them all!
He sat upon his snowy horse, and all pulled back
    So that the people could behold their kindly king.

Vernula quam facies fulvis redimita capillis
    Comptaque sub serto preradiante coma;
110   Fulget et ex auro vestis sua rubra colore,
    Que tenet interius membra venusta nimis.
Iste velud Troylus vel ut Absolon ipse decorus,
    Captivat sensum respicientis eum.
Non opus est omnem regis describere formam:
115   Regibus in cuntis non habet ille parem.
Larga decoris ei si plus natura dedisset,
    Clauderet hunc thalamis invida forte Venus!
Sistit ut in medias super arva repleta catervas,
    Nobilibus regni cingitur, ut decuit.
120   Nec procul est coniux, regina suis comitata:
    Anna sibi nomen; re sit et Anna, precor.
Pulchra quidem pulcris stat circumcincta puellis;
    Vincit Amazonibus Troia Novella sub hiis.
Sternitur ex gemmis nitidis sparsim sua vestis
125   Ad capud a planta; nil nisi gemma patet!
Nulla deest adamas, carbunculus, atque berillus:
    Qui lapis est precii, sternitur inde capud.
Quod nitet in fronte nitida radiatque per aures
    Verberat obtuitum, ne foret inde satur.
130   Aurea rex dum frena trahit et sistere cogit
    Dextrarium, proceres mox populusque silent.
Accessit propius custos, secumque togati;
    Claves leva manus, dextra tenet gladium,
Ad se converso puncto mucronis; ad instar
135   Tristis captivi, sic sua verba refert:
"En, rex, cuius ut est nimium metuenda potestas,
    Sic et amanda nimis, nec reverenda minus:
En, humiles cives, vestris pedibus provoluti,
    Reddunt se vobis et sua cunta simul.
140   Clavibus hiis gladioque, renunciat urbs modo sponte:
    Vestre voluntati prompta subesse venit.   *[fol. 9va]*
Hoc rogat assidue, lacrimis madefacta deintus,
    Mitis ut in cameram rex velit ire suam.
Non laceret, non dilaniet pulcherrima regni
145   Menia, nam sua sunt, quicquid et exstat in hiis.
Non oderit thalamum sponsus quem semper amavit;

A maiden too, her face enclosed by yellow hair,
   Her tresses neatly set beneath a garland's gleam;
110   Her red dress shines in color, brightened by the gold,
   Concealing underneath her very pretty limbs.
And he, so fair, like Troilus or Absolon,
   Makes captive all the hearts of those that see him there.
There is no need to itemize the king's good looks:
115   Among all kings on earth he clearly has no peer.
If lavish Nature had increased his beauty more,
   Then jealous Venus might have locked him in her room!
He halted in the crowded fields among the hosts,
   Surrounded fittingly by England's noble lords.
120   His wife, the queen, is near with all her retinue:
   Her name is Anne; I pray she may be Anne in deed.
She's beautiful, with other beauties all around;
   Led by such Amazons, New Troy is unsurpassed.
Her dress is strewn and overspread with gleaming gems
125   From head to toe; there's nothing visible but gems!
Carbuncle, adamant, and beryl, all are there:
   Her head is overspread with every precious stone.
What shines upon her face and gleams upon her ears
   Assaults the viewer's gaze, and leaves it wanting more.
130   The king pulls back the golden reins and halts his steed;
   At this the people and the nobles all fall still.
The warden then draws near, with aldermen in robes;
   His left hand holds the keys, his right hand holds a sword,
Its point toward himself. Just like a prisoner,
135   With woeful face, he spoke his speech as follows here:
"Your majesty, whose awful power is to be feared
   And also to be loved, and equally revered,
Behold: your humble citizens, beneath your feet
   Surrender all they have and their own selves to you.
140   With keys and sword the city gives up willingly:
   It comes all ready to surrender to your will.
Suffused with tears within, it earnestly entreats
   The king to enter in his room in gentleness.
Let him not rend or tear apart his realm's fair walls,
145   For they are his, and all that still remains inside.
Let not the bridegroom hate the room he's always loved;

Nulla subest causa cur minuatur amor."
Sumit ad hec gladium, claves quoque, Londoniarum;
    Rex cito militibus tradit utrosque suis:
150   "Acceptamus," ait, "tam vos quam reddere vestrum,
    Et placet ornatus exhibitus michi nunc,
Sed quid in urbe mea geritur modo tendo videre,
    Si scierit regem gens mea nosse suum."
Transit et interea custos, comitatus eisdem
155   Sex quater, et sistunt regia terga retro.
Reginam propius veniunt, humili quoque vultu.
    Valde precantur eam, spondet et ipsa bonum.
Corde favet, sed valde dolet quia regis in iram
    Urbs tam clara ruit, "Spes tamen exstat," ait.

160   HIIS (VELUD EST dictum) gestis, properatur ad urbem;
    Ars artem sequitur: est prior ultima nunc.
Ut valor est artis, retinet loca digna valori:
    Gaudet honore suo quelibet atque gradu.
Nigris, purpureis, albis, fulvis bene tinctis,
165   Viridibus, rubris, puniceisque togis
Ac bipartitis; sunt vestibus atque phalangis
    Artes distincte, quod decet artifices.
Illa prius, hec posterius, ars tendit ad urbem;
    Vix exercitui sufficiebat iter!
170   Turba premit turbam; iacet hic, ruit hic, cadit ille.
    [. . . . . . .]
Musica nulla tacet: cantus, strepitus, neque clangor;
    Altaque concussit ethera dulce melos,
Dumque chori fratrum psallunt regemque salutant;
    Incipit amplecti mox venerando cruces.
175   Basia dat crucibus; imitatur eum sua coniux;
    Et rogat ut regnum servet uterque deus.
T[u]nc respirare cepit tristis prius aura,
    Tempestas etenim turbinis ante fuit.
Sic pluerat (quod tristis erat); tunc sexus uterque
180   Turbari metuens turbine tam valido;
Ast Nothus ut distat, lenisque Favonius astat,
    Aura serena micat: urbs modo nil trepidat.
Strata foras urbem, qua pulcra suburbia restant —

No cause remains by which his love should be reduced."
With this, he takes up London's sword and keys as well;
    The king then hands both keys and sword to his own knights:
150 "We take you in, and your surrender, willingly;
    The fine display you've shown is pleasing to me too,
But next I plan to see what London's doing now,
    And if my people know how to accept their king."
Meanwhile the warden goes, surrounded by these four
155   Times six companions; they stand behind the king.
They come up to the queen with humble countenance,
    Beseeching her, and she prays good for them in turn.
Her heart loves them, but grieves that such a famous town
    Had earned the royal wrath, but "Hope remains," she said.

160 THIS DONE (AS has been said), they hasten to the town;
    Guilds follow guilds in line: the first becomes the last.
They keep their proper place according to their state:
    Each one rejoices in its honor and its rank.
They're dressed in robes of black, of purple, and of grey
165   (Well dyed), of green and red and scarlet too,
And bi-colored; the guilds are set apart by clothes
    And into companies, as fitting to their trades.
One first, another next, the guilds proceed to town;
    The road was scarcely big enough to hold the host!
170 Crowd jostles crowd; one lies, one trips, one falls
    [. . . . . . .]
The music's never still: the song, the roar, and shout;
    The pleasing melody strikes all the air above,
While choruses of friars sing and greet the king;
    He clasps the crosses to him, showing reverence.
175 He presses them with kisses, and his wife does too
    And both send prayers to God to keep and save the realm.
The gloomy climate then began to breathe again,
    For up to then the weather had been full of storms.
It had rained so (since it was sad); and man and wife
180   Feared lest they be upset by such a raging storm;
But when the south wind left and gentle west wind blew,
    The atmosphere shone bright: the city now was calm.
Outside the city lies a street where suburbs spread

Hec "opus Australe" dicitur — est etenim.

185   Obviat hic regi vir, in exilium modo missus,   [*fol. 9vb*]

      Arboreamque crucem fert, homicida reus.

Pronus ut ante pedes iacuit prostratus equinos,

      Flens rogitat veniam: rex sibi donat eam;

Sicque pium miseri miseret solitum misereri,

190   Gracia quam tribuit restituatur ei!

Aurea regine super erigitur capud Anne

      Pulcra corona — parum non valet illa, putes!

Mirificum opus hoc lapidum radiosa venustas

      Ditat, et eximiam efficit illa lucem.

195   Grata fuit facies vario redimita monili;

      Cultus enim patrie pulcrius ornat eam.

Pontis ut usque pedem propiat rex, stant ibi cives

      Dextrariique duo, inclita dona nimis.

Purpura cum bisso tegit hos partita caballos:

200   Cesar honorifice supra sederet eos!

Hos ducit ad regem custos deputatus in urbe,

      Urbis et ex parte talia verba refert:

"Rex pie, rex prudens, rex pacifice, dominator:

      Nil nisi pax petitur vestra — rogamus eam!

205   En, ligios vestros, letos foris, intus ovantes,

      Gaudia magna nimis hiis tulit ista dies,

Quod ducitis dignum thalamum iam visere vestrum;

      Quas valet urbs grates tota referre cupit.

Sed quia quicquid habet nimis [est] parvum dare regi,

210   Hos tamen optat equos vestra manus capiat.

Dantur in hoc signum, quod se reddunt modo cives:

      Corpora, divicias, Pergama, queque sua.

In vestris manibus sit eorum vitaque morsque,

      Et regat ad libitum regia virga suos."

215   Rex, contentus ad hec, "Et nos," ait, "ista placenter

      Munera suscipimus: iraque nostra cadit.

Concedimus pacem genti que restat in urbe;

      Plebs mea nunc erit hec, rex et ero sibi nunc."

Hec ut ait, vultu solido satis atque sereno,

220   Letificat mestos vox ea mille viros.

Ordine consimili, coniux ubi regia pausat,

      Pergitur, et custos taliter inquit ei:

Quite splendidly — its name is Southwark, "southern work."
185 The king here meets a man, a felon, homicide,
Now banished from the realm; he bears a wooden cross.
He lays himself headlong before the horses' feet
And weeping begs for pardon, which the king then grants;
Thus, kindly, he bestows his kindness on this wretch,
190 So may the grace that he has shown be shown to him!
A fine and golden crown is raised above the head
Of Anne, our queen — you can be sure it wasn't cheap!
The glowing beauty of its stones enhanced this work,
And so the crown produced a wondrous gleaming light.
195 Her face was pleasing, girt with varied necklaces;
Her country's fashion beautifies her all the more.
The king draws near the bridge's pier, where stand arrayed
The citizens, two destriers, and splendid gifts.
These horses' covering is purple slashed with white:
200 An emperor with honor would bestride these steeds!
The city's chosen warden leads them to the king
And, speaking for the city's part, recites these words:
"O kindly king, farsighted, peaceful, conqueror:
We seek for nothing but your peace — for this we beg!
205 Behold your liegemen, on the outside glad, inside
Ecstatic, for this day has brought great joy for them,
Since you now deign to come back to your marriage room;
The city's eager to give all the thanks it can.
But since its all is not enough to give a king,
210 The city begs you to accept these destriers.
They're given as a sign that Londoners now yield
Their bodies, riches, Pergamum, and all that's theirs.
Their life and death is now to be within your hands,
And may your royal rod guide subjects at its will."
215 The king, at this contented, said: "We too accept
These gifts with pleasure: now at last our wrath is gone.
We grant our peace to those that live within these walls;
They're all my people now, and now I'll be their king."
When he said this, with countenance serene and firm,
220 His words brought joy to thousands then enmired in gloom.
They go on in this way, and when the royal bride
Stops in the way, the Warden speaks to her like this:

"O generosaque nobilis imperatoria proles,
   Stipite nata quidem magnifici generis.
225 Vos deus elegit, ad sceptra Britannica digne:
   Imperii consors estis, et apta fore.
Flectere regales poterit regina rigores,
   Mitis ut in gentem rex velit esse suam.
Mollit amore virum mulier: deus huic dedit illam.
230 Tendat ad hoc vester, o pia, dulcis amor!   *[fol. 10ra]*
Leta cupit faciem plebs hec modo cernere vestram,
   In qua consistunt et salus et sua spes.
En, presentat equm vobis, licet hoc minus equo
   Extiterit donum, corde tamen hillari.
235 Est nam qui teneros vestros leviter ferat artus;
   Ambulat et numquam cespitat in phaleris.
Partiti tegitur equs hic ex veste coloris
   Purpurei bissi — sic fuerant reliqui.
Accipiat domina (modicum licet) hoc modo munus:
240 Supplicat instanter integra nostra cohors."
Suscipit illa datum, grates referendo benignas,
   Spondet et auxilium quod valet illa suum.
Voce licet tenui loqueretur et ut muliebri,
   Grata tamen facies urbis amica fuit.

245 TALITER HIIS gestis, gaudenter itur in urbem;
   Turba premit turbam, sic iter artat eam.
Venit ut ad portam pontis regina, patenter
   Sors bona prodigium mox dedit, ecce, novum:
Namque sequntur eam currus duo, cum dominabus;
250 Rexerat hos Pheton; unus enim cecidit.
Femina feminea sua dum sic femina nudat,
   Vix poterat risum plebs retinere suum.
Casus et ille placet, veniat (rogo) quod michi signat,
   Corruat ut luxus et malus omnis amor!
255 Pergitur hinc; rutilant, fulgent, splendentque platee:
   Omnibus in vicis plauditur et canitur.
Spectantur pulcre, dum spectant ista, puelle,
   Nulla fenestra fuit, has nisi que tenuit.
Virgineas facies qui cerneret urbis in alto,
260 Quod decus est ymo sperneret ut nichilum.

"O noble high-born lady, born of lofty race,
    Imperial in rank, renowned in family.

225 God chose you, worthily, for Britain's sceptered rule:
    You share in her broad rule, as you are fit to do.

The queen is able to deflect the king's firm rule,
    So he will show a gentle face to his own folk.

A woman soothes a man by love: God gave him her.

230   O gentle Anne, let your sweet love be aimed at this!

These happy people now desire to see your face,
    For in it all their well-being and hope reside.

Behold, they offer you a horse, and though the gift
    Is less than fair, it's given with a happy heart.

235 It's of a type to gently bear your tender limbs;
    It ambles and it never stumbles in its gear.

This horse is covered with a cloth of double hue
    Of white and purple — so were all the others too.

Now, may your ladyship accept this gift (though small):

240   Our company together begs you earnestly."

She takes the gift, and thanks them for it gratefully,
    And pledges to them all the help that she can give.

Although her words were in a woman's voice and soft,
    Her pleasing face, however, was the city's friend.

245 THESE THINGS thus done, they joyfully proceed to town;
    Crowd jostles crowd, for so the route compresses them.

The queen came to the bridge's gate, and then good luck
    Provided suddenly a new astonishment:

Two carriages, packed full with ladies, followed her;

250   A Phaeton was their driver; one was overturned.

When women thus exposed their female thighs to view,
    The people scarcely could restrain a hearty laugh.

So may this lucky fall's significance come true,
    And lechery and lustful passion come to grief!

255 The march proceeds; in splendor public squares shine bright:
    In all the streets the singing and the cheers resound.

The pretty girls look on, and they are looked at too,
    For all the windows were packed full with pretty girls.

Whoever in the high street saw these maidens' looks

260   Would scorn what's "beautiful" as though it had no worth.

Quippe satis lento passu transitur in urbe,
    Concursu populi prepediente viam.
At ubi perventum medium fuit urbis et usque
    Introitum vici, dicitur ille "Forum,"
265   Quales texture picturarumque figure,
    Qualis et ornatus scribere quis poterit?
Nempe videtur ibi, de summis usque deorsum,
    Nil nisi divicie, vultus et angelici.
Stillat aqueductus Bachum — nec adest ibi Tetis! —
270   Rubra dat ille liquor pocula mille viris.
Huius et in tecto steterat quasi celicus ordo,
    Qui canit angelicos, arte iuvante, melos.
Densa velud folia seu flores, sic volat aurum,
    Undique virginea discuciente manu.
275   Itur abhinc; mediam dum rex venit usque plateam,   *[fol. 10rb]*
    Cernit ibi castrum, stat: stupet hinc nimium.
Pendula per funes est fabrica totaque turris,
    Etheris et medium vendicat illa locum;
Stant et in hac turri iuvenis formosaque virgo,
280   Hic velud angelus est, hec coronata fuit.
Cerneret has facies quisquis, puto, non dubitaret
    Nil fore sub celo quod sibi plus placeat.
Rex reginaque tunc astant, bene discucientes
    Quid velit hec turris alta vel hii iuvenes.
285   Descendunt ab ea iuvenis, simul ipsaque virgo;
    Nulla fuit scala, nec patuere gradus.
Nubibus inclusi veniunt, et in ethere pendent,
    Quo tamen ingenio nescio, crede michi!
Iste tenet ciphum; geminas gerit illa coronas.
290   Hec nitidis gemmis; plenus et iste mero.
Hec rutilante novo fabricata quidem satis auro
    Singula testatur fulgida materies.
Materiam superavit opus: patet hoc et in artis
    Et simul artificis subtilitate nova.
295   Optulit ergo suas custodi virgo coronas;
    Quas in utraque manu, sic el[o]quendo, tenet:
"Rex," ait, "illustris reginaque nobilis, ambos
    Custodiat semper vos deus incolumes!
Qui dat terreni vobis dyademata regni

64

They pass throughout the city at a gentle pace,
  For crowds of people block the route along the way.
But when they reached the middle of the town, just where
  The street begins that's known in English as "The Cheap,"
265 Who could describe the tapestries and tableaux there,
  And all the decoration and the fine displays?
For there was nothing to be seen, from top to toe,
  But lavishness and faces such as angels have.
An aqueduct dripped Bacchus — Tethys wasn't there! —
270   That potion poured a ruby drink to thousands there.
On this house roof there stood a heavenly array,
  Which sang angelic songs, with art's assisting aid.
Gold flies around like leaves and blossoms, thick and fast,
  For everywhere a maiden's hand spreads it around.
275 They left; and when the king had reached the central square,
  He saw a castle there: he stopped and was amazed.
The total structure and its tower hung from ropes,
  And occupied a space suspended in the air;
Within the tower stood a youth in angel form,
280   A girl beside him, beautiful, who wore a crown.
Whoever saw their forms, I think, would have no doubt
  That nothing underneath the sun could please him more.
The king and queen then paused, reflecting on this sight
  And what the tower means and who the young ones were.
285 They now descend, the young man and the girl as well;
  There was no ladder, nor could any steps be seen.
They came enwrapped in clouds, suspended in the air,
  But what device was used, believe me, I don't know!
The young man holds a cup; the girl extends two crowns.
290   The latter shine with gems; the cup is full of wine.
The bright material bears witness that the crowns
  Were finely fashioned out of gleaming brand new gold.
The workmanship surpassed the substance, as was shown
  By novel subtlety of artist and of art.
295 The maiden then presents the warden with the crowns;
  He holds them in each hand, and then he speaks these words:
"O king illustrious and noble queen," he said,
  "May God guard both of you and keep you safe and sound!
May He, who gave you crowns of rulership on earth,

300   Regna perhennia celestia donet item!
        Cernite iam plebem vestram, quam leta salutat
           Vos et honorare gliscit, ut ipsa valet.
        Nititur ex studio (sensu quoque) quod habet omni
           Pendere nunc vobis intime quod placeat;
305   Mittit et hinc, binas vobis referendo coronas,
           Innumeras grates, si capiatis eas.
        Non decet hoc alios donum; rogitat tamen ipsa,
           Sumat ut hoc placite vestra benigna manus."
        Contentantur ad hec tam rex quam regia coniux;
310   Subridendo parum sumit uterque datum.
        Ridet et ad vinum roseum, quod ridet in auro,
           Quodque propinat ei portitor angelicus.
        Spem tulit ex ridente gena tunc plebs utriusque,
           Obsequiis animos se quietasse suos.
315   Invisis gradibus, simul angelus ipsaque virgo,
           Nubibus inclusi, mox loca prima petunt.

        USQUE MONASTERIUM Pauli cito tunc properatur,
           Cuius et ante fores mira patet species:
        Trino tronus ibi circumdatus undique giro
320   Angelici prefert ordinis effigiem,
        Angelicisque choris sic virginei sociantur,   *[fol. 10va]*
           Psallentes pariter quisque canore suo,
        Sicque micant facies iuvenum tam in hiis quam in illis,
           Fiat ut extaticus intime respiciens.
325   Nam puerilis etas iuvenum sexus utriusque
           Extat ut est maior, sedibus inferior.
        Supra sedebat eos iuvenis quasi sit deus ipse;
           Lux radiosa sibi solis ad instar inest.
        Flammigerum vultum gerit hic, niveas quoque vestes;
330   Supra ierarchias celicas ille sedet.
        Organa pulsat ibi; mentem rapit hec melodia,
           Vocibus angelicis dum canit ille chorus.
        Hinc decor, hinc dulcor: oculus recreatur, et auris:
           Singula cernentes obstupuere simul.
335   Quot putas hic musas, quot et instrumenta canora,
           Quam quoque multimodum hic genus organicum?
        Fistula, cistula, tibia, timpana cum monacordo,

300   Reward you too with heaven's everlasting realms!
       Behold your people now, how happily they greet
          You and desire to honor you, as best they can.
       They strive with all the effort (and the wit) they have
          To give to you whatever pleases you at heart;
305   And so they send to you, by giving these two crowns,
          Their countless thanks, if you will kindly take this gift.
       This gift would not be right for others; but we ask
          Your kindly hand now to accept it with good will."
       At this the king and royal bride are well content;
310   And, smiling slightly, each one takes their gift in turn.
       They smile too at the ruby wine which smiles in gold,
          And which a server with an angel's face pours out.
       The people then took hope from each one's smiling cheek,
          That by their services they'd put their minds at rest.
315   Up unseen steps the angel and the maiden rise,
          Enwrapped in clouds, and then they seek their former place.

       THEY HASTEN then towards the Minster of St. Paul's;
          Before its doors a wondrous spectacle appears:
       A throne surrounded on all sides by three big rings
320   Portrays a likeness of angelic ordinance.
       To choirs of angels virgin companies are joined
          And sing together, harmonizing in their song.
       The faces of the young shine in both these and those,
          That all that see them close are utterly enthralled.
325   The childish age of these young folk of either sex
          Shows in the bigger ones all taking lower seats.
       Above all sat a youth, as though like God himself;
          A ray of light, just like the sun, shines in this youth.
       He wears a flaming face and snow-white clothes as well;
330   He sits above the ranks of heaven's holy troops.
       A sound rings out; the melody enchants the mind,
          When with angelic voice the choir resounds in song.
       It's sweet and beautiful, refreshing ear and eye:
          Those seeing all these things were altogether stunned.
335   How many kinds of music do you think there were,
          And tuneful instruments of every shape and size?
       Pipe, citole, flute and drum and monochord were there,

Organa, psalteria, cimbala cumque lira,
Zambuce, cithare, situleque tubeque vielle,
340   Buccina cum nablis, simphonicisque choris.
Singula scripturo deerit michi sensus et hora:
Plurima namque michi sustulit ipse stupor.
Rex reginaque mox post hec pedites adierunt,
Sacra monasterii tunc visitare loca.
345   O[c]currunt pariter primas et episcopus urbis;
Obviat et clerus illius ecclesie.
Concomitantur eos, in cultu pontificali,
Ad Erkenwaldi sancta sepulcra simul.
Quippe, deo precibus sanctoque datis venerato;
350   Concito scandit equm, qui fuit ante pedes.

EST PLUS ADHUC. Transitur abhinc, in Lud quoque porta:
Consimilis cultus stat, similisque nitor.
Ad fluvii pontem, nimium bene culta refulgent
Agmina spirituum: hii quoque dulce canunt,
355   Hii dant incensum, hii psallunt, hiique salutant,
Floribus hii sternunt singula subter eos.
Ast ubi perventum fuit ad Barram cito Templi,
Silva super porte tecta locata fuit!
Hec, quasi desertum, tenuit genus omne ferarum,
360   Mixtum reptilibus, vermibus, et variis.
Sunt ibi spineta, sunt dumi, suntque rubeta;
Fraxinus et corulus, quercus et alta pirus,
Prunus, acer, pepulus, populus quoque, tilia, fagus,
Ulm[u]s, lentiscus, palma, salix tremulus;
365   Hic lupus, hic leo, pardus, et ursus, et hic monacornus,
Hic elephas, castor, simia, tigris, aper,
Hic onager, cervus celer, hic panteraque, dama,   *[fol. 10vb]*
Hic vulpes fetens, taxus, ibique lepus.
Currunt, discurrunt, pugnant, mordent, saliuntque,
370   Ut solet ad vastum bestia seva nemus.
Astitit hiis medius sanctus baptista Iohannes,
Indicat hic digito: "Agnus et ecce dei!"
Inspicit attente rex hunc quia, quem notat iste
Illius ut meminit, micior inde fuit:
375   Nam quia devotus colit hunc constanter eidem

And organs, psalteries, and cymbals, with the lyre,
    Sambukes, citerns, citoles, and trumpets, fiddles too,
340   Great horns and strings, and voices all in harmony.
    For me to write all this, both wit and time would fail:
        Amazement drove so many things quite from my mind.
    Soon after this the king and queen went forth on foot
        To pay a visit to the abbey's holy site.
345   The primate and the city's bishop met them there;
        A cleric of that church came out to greet them too.
    These three, in bishop's robes, escort the king and queen
        Together, to the holy tomb of Erkenwald.
    They pray to God and to the saint they all revere;
350   He swiftly mounts the horse that stands before his feet.

THERE'S MORE to come. They leave from here, and at Lud's gate
    A similar display is shown, and just as fine.
    There, at the river bridge, the hosts of spirits shine,
        All well decked out and dressed: and they sing sweetly too.
355   Some sprinkle incense, others dance, and some salute,
        And some spread flowers everywhere beneath their feet.
    Then soon they finally arrive at Temple Bar,
        And there a forest had been placed atop the gate!
    It had, just like a desert, every kind of beast,
360   Including reptiles, snakes, and many other kinds.
    There brakes and briar-patches spread, and thorny shrubs,
        An ash, a hazelbush, an oak, a lofty pear,
    A plum, a maple, bullace, poplar, lime and beech,
        Elm, mastic-bush, and palm and quaking willow-tree;
365   Wolf, lion, leopard, bear, and unicorn were there,
        A beaver, elephant, ape, tiger, and a boar,
    Wild ass, swift deer, a panther, and a doe were there,
        A smelly fox, a badger, and a hare as well.
    They run and run around, they fight and bite and leap,
370   As savage beasts behave in desert wilderness.
    Amidst them all the holy John the Baptist stood,
        And pointed with his finger: "Look, the Lamb of God!"
    The king observed him closely, since, remembering
        The saint that was portrayed, his manner grew more mild:
375   For, since he honored him devotedly, to him

Pre reliquis sanctis porrigit ipse preces.
Huius ad intuitum, si quid sibi manserat ire,
Extitit extinctum protinus usque nichil.
Angelus a tecto descendens mox satis alto,
380 Splendida dona nimis fert in utraque manu,
Sunt etenim tabule, sacris altaribus apte:
Quas nequit inspiciens immemor esse dei.
Inde crucifixi Christi stat sculpta figura,
Discipuli flentis, matris et extatice;
385 Sculpitur hic et uterque latro, velud in cruce pendens:
Ut deus est passus, tota patet series.
Quod minus extat in hiis, quod vilius, hoc fuit aurum:
Multimodis gemmis pingitur istud opus.
Non fuerant vise tabule prius orbis in amplo
390 Que deceant velud hec tam bene sceptrigeram.
Sumit ab angelicis manibus tabulas modo dictas
Custos, sicque sua publice verba refert:
"Salve, pater populi! Rex, dux, princeps, modo salve!
Salvet et omnipotens vos deus, alma salus!
395 Quam fuit hec preclara dies hiis civibus, in qua
Constituit regem vos deus esse suum!
Prole patrissante — Ricardi quod fuit ante
Nomen adhuc repetit quicquid honoris erat.
Regibus ergo probis patribusque bonis bona proles
400 Successura fuit: sors dedit ut decuit.
Nobilitas generis, virtus proba, formaque pulcra,
Gracia, prosperitas, ingeniumque sagax:
Queque decent regem, persona simul capit una —
Una, procul dubio, non nisi vestra, scio!
405 Sed, super hec, pietas compassio veraque cordis,
Dignificans animum, vos probat esse probum.
Spes etenim populi pocior fit, [u]t ad pietatem
(Qua datur hiis venia) regis et ira cadit.
Significant satis hoc tabule quas cernitis iste:
410 Quas regi pia plebs optulit, ecce, pio.
Orat ut inspiciat has, rex cum tangitur ira,
Mortis et ut Christi mox velit esse memor;
Parcat et ignaris, veluti rex celicus ille, [*fol. 11ra*]
Hostibus indulgens, semper inultus erat.

70

He offered prayers before all other holy saints.
On seeing him, if any anger still remained,
    It vanished utterly, expiring on the spot.
From off the lofty roof an angel then came down,
380   And in each hand he carried very splendid gifts,
For these were tablets, suited to an altar place:
    No one who looked at these could fail to think of God.
A carving was displayed of Christ upon the Cross,
    A sad disciple, and a mother, quite distraught;
385 Two thieves were sculpted too, appearing crucified:
    The total sequence showed the suffering of God.
The meanest and most cheap material was gold:
    The work was finely dressed with gems of every kind.
In all the world no tablets had been seen like these
390   So fittingly to suit a scepter-bearing hand.
The warden took the tablets from the angel's hands
    And thus in public made the speech that follows here:
"Hail, father of the people! King, prince, leader, hail!
    May God almighty, kindly health, keep you all the while!
395 How splendid was that day for London's citizens,
    The day when God appointed you to be their king!
As father, so the son — King Richard's name repeats
    His ancestor's and all the honor it entails.
To good and noble kings and ancestors, his line
400   Was sure to correspond: faith granted what was right.
Innate nobility, great bravery, good looks,
    Grace and prosperity, and wit and wisdom too:
All these, things that befit a king, one person holds —
    One person, as I know for sure, and that is you!
405 Above all this, your piety and empathy,
    Heartfelt, which show your mind, proclaim your probity.
The people's hope is greater still, when royal wrath
    Subsides and turns to mercy, pardoning them all.
These tablets that you see are symbols of all this:
410   Your faithful people give them to their faithful king.
They beg the king, when touched by wrath, to look upon
    These tablets and reflect upon the death of Christ;
And spare the ignorant, as heaven's king once did,
    Forgiving enemies, and always unavenged.

71

415   Principis est potuisse suas extendere vires
        In tamen externos, quos oderit, populos.
    Rex et apum caret omnis acu, tamen extat eo plus
        Sponte timendus ab hiis quos ferit ipse nichil!
    Sumat et hinc vestra manus hoc modicum modo munus,
420   In signum pacis quam rogat hic populus!"
    Extendendo manum, rex tunc sacra munera tangens.
        "Pax," ait, "huic urbi, civibus atque meis!
    Intuitu Christi, matrisque sue generose,
        Baptisteque Iohannis, michi precipui,
425   Necnon sanctorum quorum modo cerno figuras,
        Sponte remitto mee crimina cunta plebis!
    Sed veniatis," ait, "ad nostra palacia cuncti:
        Plenus enim finis — pax quoque — fiet ibi."
    Rex transit; regina venit; conformia custos
430   Munera presentans intulit ista sibi:
    "Inclita Cesareo soboles propagata parente,
        Quam decor et forma nobilitant nimium,
    Matris christifere nomen sortita Marie,
        Quod titulis, Anna, 'gracia' sonat idem.
435   Non decet hunc titulum vacuum fore, nam gerit illum
        Gracia que populis nunc valet esse suis.
    Vos ideo meminisse decet, pia dux dominarum,
        Sanguinis et generis nominis et proprii.
    Grata loqui pro gente sua regina valebit —
440   Quod vir non audet sola potest mulier.
    Hester ut Assueri trepidans stetit ante tribunal,
        Irritat edicta que prius ipse tulit.
    Nec dubium quin ob hoc vos omnipotens dedit huius
        Participem regni, sitis ut Hester ei.
445   Propterea, petit urbs vestrum prostrata benignum
        Auxilium, in quo plus habet ipsa spei.
    Donat et has vobis tabulas, altaribus aptas:
        Ut stent ante deum, vos tamen ante virum.
    Cernitis has quociens, tociens meminisse velitis
450   Urbis, et efficere rex sit amicus ei."
    Illa refert grates nimias pro munere tanto:
        "In me, si quid erit, perficietur," ait.

415   A prince has power to extend his might abroad,
        But just against whatever foreigners he hates.
    In bees the king's without a sting, but all the more
        He must be feared by those he doesn't strike at all!
    So may your hand accept this gift, although it's small,
420   To signify the peace that all your people beg!"
    The king stretched out his hand and touched the sacred gifts.
      "Let there be peace to London and my citizens!"
    He said. "For Christ and for His noble mother too,
      For John the Baptist, my own saint and special friend,
425   For all the saints whose figures I now contemplate,
      I grant forgiveness gladly for my people's crimes!
    But to my palace all of you must come," he said,
      "For there a final end will come — and also peace."
    The king passed by; the queen arrived; the warden gave
430   Her matching gifts and, as he did, he said these words:
    "Famed offspring of a father born from Caesar's line,
      Ennobled greatly by your beauty and your grace,
    Who bears the name of Mary's mother, Mary who
      Bore Christ — the name of Anna means the same as 'grace.'
435   This name should not be meaningless, for it is hers
      Who now for all her people can display her grace.
    You, kindly ladies' leader, ought to call to mind
      Your blood and family and your own proper name.
    A queen can, for her people, speak the words that please —
440   None but a woman can do what no man would dare.
    When fearful Hesther stood before King Assuer's throne,
      She brought to naught the edicts that the king had passed.
    For this, no doubt, almighty God gave you to be
      A partner in this reign, a Hesther for the realm.
445   Therefore your people's city, prostrate, begs your help
      And kindness, for on these it mainly puts its hope.
    It gives to you these tablets, fit for altar place:
      They stand in front of God, as you before your man.
    Whenever you see these, you'll gladly call to mind
450   Your city and ensure the king remains its friend."
    She gives her heartfelt thanks for such a splendid gift:
      "Whatever's in my power," she said, "it will be done."

ITUR ABHINC, CUNTIS equitantibus ordine pulcro;
    Westquemonasterium, rege iubente, petunt.
455   Quis fuit ornatus aule, quis cultus ibidem,
        Scribere difficile, nec reserare leve.
    Nam ea textrili fuit arte domus cooperta
        Tam prius insolita quod stupet intuitus.   *[fol. 11rb]*
    Summa tenet summi tronus regis loca scamni,
460   Aurea tegmina quem splendida sola tegunt.
    Sceptriger hoc nitidum scandit rex, ecce, tribunal;
        Circumstant proceres, moxque silere iubent.
    Ingreditur regina, suis comitata puellis,
        Pronaque regales corruit ante pedes.
465   Erigitur, mandante viro. "Quid," ait, "petis, Anna?
        Exprime, de votis expediere tuis."
    "Dulcis," ait, "mi rex, michi vir, michi vis, michi vita!
        Dulcis amor, sine quo vivere fit michi mors!
    Regibus in cuntis, similem quis possidet urbem,
470   Que velud hec hodie magnificaret eum?
    Quis cultus, quis honor, qui sumptus, munera quanta,
        Sunt inpensa modo, rex venerande, tibi!
    Nos quoque mortales et, ut hii, velud umbra caduci
        Simus in hiis mortis absit ut immemores!
475   Quo maiorem sumit honorem, quisquis eo plus
        Est humilis et erit, si sapiens fuerit.
    Hinc, mi rex, mi dulcis amor, memor esse velitis —
        Supplico prostrata — quid modo contigerit.
    Tempora post Bruti regumque peracta priorum
480   (Quamvis et Arthurus annumeretur eis),
    Non fuerat cuiquam regi datus hic morituro
        Tantus honor, quantum contulit ista dies.
    Maior enim si facta foret reverencia regi,
        Tangeret iniuria publica forte deum!
485   Hinc, super hos cives, super urbem sic reverentem,
        Tam vos quam vestros, intime condoleo;
    Et rogo constanter, per eum quem fertis amorem
        Ad me, condignum si quid amore gero,
    Parcere dignemini plebibus, qui tanta dedere
490   Munera, tam prompte nobis ad obsequia;
    Et placeat veteri nunc urbem reddere iuri

THEN ALL depart on horseback in their fine array;
   And, at the king's command, to Westminster they go.
455   The decoration of the hall and its array
   Would be no easy task to tell or to unfold.
The house was overspread with all the weaver's skill;
   The gaze was stunned at such an unaccustomed sight.
The royal throne has pride of place upon the dais,
460   Bedecked with coverings of nothing but fine gold.
The scepter-wielding king then mounts the gleaming throne;
   The nobles stand there, urging silence on the crowd.
The queen comes in, accompanied by all her maids,
   And falls, bowed down, prostrate, before the royal feet.
465   At his command she stands. "What, Anna, do you seek?"
   He asks. "Just speak, and your desires will be met."
"Sweet king of mine," she said, "my man, my strength, my life!
   Sweet love, without whom life to me would be like death!
What king on earth rules such a city that, like this
470   Today, would honor him and magnify his name?
What worship, honor, what expense, what splendid gifts
   Have just today, most honored king, been spent on you!
We too, like these, are mortal, fleeting like a shade:
   May God forbid that we should give no thought to death!
475   The greater honor one receives, if he is wise,
   The more humility he has and always shall.
And so, my king, my sweetest love, please keep in mind —
   I beg you on my knees — what has just happened here.
Since Brutus' days and those of ancient kings
480   (If even Arthur were included in their ranks),
Such honor never has been shown to mortal king
   As has, this day, been granted and conferred on you.
If greater reverence were shown towards the king,
   The public wrong, perhaps, would trouble God himself!
485   Thus, for these citizens, for this respectful town,
   For you yourself and yours, I feel the deepest grief
And beg you earnestly, by that love that you have
   For me, if I do anything to earn your love,
Please deign to spare these people, who have given you
490   Such gifts, so readily, in service to us both;
And please restore the city to its ancient rights

Ac libertates restituisse suas."
"Sumo placenter," ait tunc rex, "carissima coniux,
    Queque petita modo: nec nego quod rogitas.
495   Consessura mecum scandas, dulcissima, tronum,
    Namque loquar populo paucula verba meo."
Sedibus ut teneros regina sedens locat artus.
    Rege loquente; duces, plebs quoque, tota silet.
"Vos," ait, "o cives, vos regia gens specialis,
500   Nostri quos aliis plus refovere patres:
Vobis in hoc regno nullos fore liberiores
    Constat, et extollit vos favor hic nimium.   [*fol. 11va*]
Propter opes nimias, magnos quoque propter honores,
    Degenerasse potest urbs mea forte modo.
505   Nunc ubi sunt iuste leges, ubi rectaque iura?
    Quo timor in dominos? Quo modo fugit amor?
Quo bona nunc pietas? Inopum proteccio grata?
    Quo socialis amor? Omnis abhinc periit.
Quippe potest tante fieri modo causa ruine,
510   Que generat fastum, tam bona prosperitas.
Quod ego si scirem — sciat urbs hec, nam bene sciret —
    Urbibus in reliquis non foret ista prior.
Antiquus tamen ille favor, quem pristina regum
    Approbat auctoritas, non minuetur adhuc,
515   Sentit enim vestrum mea mens per signa timorem,
    Vos quoque spero per hoc ad meliora trahi.
Sumptus enim video vestros, data munera penso,
    Coniugis atque mee pondero valde preces.
Vos ideoque cavete deinceps principis iras;
520   Contemptu proceres non habetote meos.
Antiquam servate fidem. Nova dogmata semper
    Spernite, que veteres non didicere patres.
Ecclesiam quoque catholicam defendite totam:
    Non habet illa gradum, quin colat ipse deum.
525   Iudicibus vestris insit timor omnipotentis;
    Pauperis in causam fraus mala ne veniat;
Sit et in urbe mea bona pax — contencio nulla,
    Nec conventiculum federis insoliti.
Si nostras etenim rumor penetraverit aures
530   Obvius hiis monitis, urbs luet — haud dubium!

And give it back at last its former liberties."
"My dearest wife," the king said then, "I gladly take
    To heart what you have asked: I won't deny your boon.
495   Come up, my sweetest, to the throne and sit with me,
    For to my people I must speak a word or two."
The queen then placed her tender limbs upon the seat.
    The king began; the nobles and the folk fell still.
"O citizens, my people, special to the king,
500   On whom my ancestors bestowed especial care:
It's sure that in this realm none more than you enjoyed
    Such liberties, our favor raised you up so high.
From such prosperity, and splendid honors too,
    My city might, perhaps, be now degenerate.
505   Where now are laws and edicts that are fair and just?
    What has become of fear of lords? Where has love fled?
Where now is piety? Protection of the poor?
    Where is its loving friendship? All has passed away.
The cause of such a recent fall perhaps might be
510   This great prosperity, which is a sense of pride.
If I know this — let London know, for so it would —
    It would not be the first among all other towns.
Yet ancient favor, which antique authority
    Of kings approves, will not now be decreased as yet,
515   For in my mind, from all these signs, I feel your fear
    And hope that thus you are now drawn to better things.
I see what you have spent; I weigh the gifts you've made
    And also take account of pleadings from my wife.
So, citizens, henceforth beware the prince's wrath;
520   Don't scorn or hold my lords and nobles in contempt.
Observe the ancient law. Reject for evermore
    New doctrines that the ancient fathers did not learn.
Also defend and guard the total catholic church:
    It has no sacred rank that does not worship God.
525   Let all your judges hold the Lord in awe;
    Let no misuse or fraudulence afflict the poor;
And in my city let there be fair peace — not strife,
    And no newfangled gatherings in novel leagues.
If any news should reach me that conflicts with this
530   Advice, the city will regret it — mark my words!

Sed modo suscipite claves, gladium quoque vestrum,
   Legibus antiquis hanc regitote plebem.
Antea quod licuit, liceat modo, dum tamen equm
   Extiterit, solitum non variando modum.
535   Premineat maior, electus qui regat urbem,
   Regis et, ut solito, suppleat ille vices.
Vos quoque, felices dulci iam pace potiti,
   Pergite gaudentes ad loca quisque sua!"

GAUDET AD HEC turba, prostrata ruit, iacet humo,
540   Acclamat laudes vocibus altisonis:
"Vivat rex! Vivat semper! Vivat bene! Vivat!
   Longa sit in regno sospite vita suo!
Sint sibi felices anni mensesque diesque,
   Floreat et victis hostibus ipse suis!"
545   Dumque strepunt, abeunt, redeunt, regem benedicunt,
   Exitus est operi terminus iste rei.

But now take back your keys, receive your sword again,
    And henceforth rule this people by your ancient laws.
What was before allowed, is now allowed again,
    As long as it is fair, not straying from the norm.
535   A chosen mayor should be above, to rule the town,
    And, as is usual, to act the role of king.
You too, now blest (since you have won the peace you sought),
    Go joyfully, each one, returning to your homes!"

AT THIS THE crowd rejoice and fall prostrate and lie
540   On earth, and sing out praise in voices to the skies:
"Long live the king, live long, live safe and well, long live the king!
    Long may he reign, and may his realm be well!
May all his years and months and days be blessed ones,
    And may he flourish, quelling all his enemies!"
545   And while they shout and come and go and bless the king,
    The end of this affair brings closure to this work.

Explanatory Notes

3–6   Cicero, *De amicitia* 23.88, in *De senectute, De amicitia, De divinatione*, ed. and trans. William Armistead Falconer (Cambridge, MA: Harvard University Press, 1923), pp. 194–95: "Verum ergo illud est, quod a Tarentino Archyta, ut opinor, dici solitum nostros senes commemorare audivi ab aliis senibus auditum: si quis in caelum ascendisset naturamque mundi et pulchritudinem siderum perspexisset, insuavem illam admirationem ei fore, quae iucundissima fuisset, si aliquem cui narraret habuisset. Sic natura solitarium nihil amat semperque ad aliquod tamquam adminiculum adnititur, quod in amicissimo quoque dulcissimum est" ["True, therefore, is that celebrated saying of Archytas of Tarentum, I think it was — a saying that I have heard repeated by our old men who in their turn heard it from their elders. It is to this effect: 'If a man should ascend alone into heaven and behold clearly the structure of the universe and the beauty of the stars, there would be no pleasure for him in the awe-inspiring sight, which would have filled him with delight if he had had someone to whom he could describe what he had seen.' Thus nature, loving nothing solitary, always strives for some sort of support, and man's best support is a very dear friend"]. Maidstone's *Determinacio* begins similarly (ed. Edden, p. 121), with an anecdote from Plato.

9   *Ricarde*. Unidentified, but certainly not (*ut puto*) King Richard; see the Introduction, p. 33 and note 91.

11   *Trenovantum*. I.e., London; compare lines 18 ("Nova Troia"), 39 ("Troia"), 123 ("Troia Novella"), and 212 ("Pergama"). On these allusions, see Federico, "A Fourteenth-Century Erotics of Politics."

15–16 I.e., the year 1392.

17   *soror*. I.e., Diana, the Roman lunar deity. Counting from March (when the new year traditionally began), the moon had completed its monthly cycle (*Phebo fuerat soror associata*) six times (*bis ter*) by August.

19–20 I.e., 21 August.

22   *Perfida Lingua.* I.e., *Male-bouche*, a *Roman de la rose*-like personification, of a sort that Chaucer's early work (including the English verse translation of the *Roman*) had domesticated; compare line 41.

29   *quot mortes.* Probably a specific reference to the legal murders of various adherents of the king, including Robert Tresilian and Simon Burley, by the so-called Merciless Parliament in February and March 1388, in the aftermath of the Appellants' coup; see Saul, *Richard II*, pp. 191–94.

30   *Quamque sit inultus.* Evidently written before events of 1397 and left unrevised; see Barron, "The Tyranny of Richard II."

35   This claim is contradicted by the so-called Articles of Deposition of 1399; see Eberle, "The Politics of Courtly Style," especially p. 172.

45   *Urbis custodem.* Baldwin Raddington — a nephew of Richard's late lamented intimate Simon Burley, possibly alluded to at line 29 — was appointed warden of London by the king 22 July 1392, in succession to Edward Dallingridge, the first *custos*, who had been appointed 25 June 1392, as part of the royal takeover of the city; see Barron, "The Quarrel of Richard II," pp. 184 and 188, and, for Raddington's career, Tout, *Chapters* 4.196–99.

47   *Regis in occursum vestri vos este parati.* Compare Matthew 24:44: "Ideo et vos estote parati, quia, qua nescitis hora, Filius hominis venturus est" ["Wherefore be you also ready, because at what hour you know not the Son of man will come" — Douay-Rheims, Challoner rev.; all Biblical citations come from this edition]; possibly recalling Isaiah 40:3: "Vox clamantis: In deserto parate viam Domini, rectas facite in solitudine semitas Dei nostri" ["The voice of one crying in the desert: Prepare ye the way of the Lord, make straight in the the wilderness the path of our God"].

52   *trans vada vadat.* I.e., cross the Thames, so leaving the city.

62   *celum.* I.e., canopy.

74   *maior.* Here equivalent to Modern English "mayor." In fact, the office was effectively suspended in the period 25 June 1392 to 13 October 1392, during the tenure of the *custodes* appointed by the king.

80   *Secta.* I.e., a suit of livery; compare line 95.

81–95   Though Maidstone uses various Latinized English and French terms in this list of London guilds, the more remarkable feature may be his frequent resort to terms from Plautine comedy (*caupo, coqus, faber, merx, piscarius, pistor* ["baker"], *sutor* ["cobbler"], *textor, tonsor, zonarius*). Maidstone's list was used as a source of vocabulary for Latham's *Revised Medieval Latin Word-List from British and Irish Sources*, from which the glosses below were mostly taken; other inferences are labeled probable. Also, it is noteworthy that Maidstone begins his list with the guilds that were the strongholds of merchant-oligarchic power, the goldsmiths, the fishmongers, the mercers, and the vintners, though in doing so he would probably only have been reflecting the order of the procession itself. The standard treatment of the history of these organizations remains Unwin, *The Gilds and Companies of London*. For various possible meanings of the demonstration of guild-solidarity that the procession represents, see Federico, "A Fourteenth-Century Erotics of Politics," especially pp. 150–51.

81   *argentarius.* Probably meaning "goldsmith," by extension (lit., "silversmith").

82   *Mercibus hic deditus.* Probably meaning "mercer."

83   *apothecarius.* Probably meaning "grocer" (lit., "apothecary").

85   *scissor.* I.e., "cloth-shearer."

86   *mango.* Probably meaning "haberdasher" (lit., "monger").

87   *archifices.* I.e., "bowyer."

91   *streparius.* Probably meaning "saddler," equivalent to *sellarius* (lit., "stirrup-maker").

93   This remark seems misplaced, coming mid-catalogue as it does here. Possibly some transposition of lines or other garbling occurred in transmission, helping to account also for what happens next: no pentameter follows to close the couplet begun in line 93, with the implication that at least a line of Maidstone's writing has been lost at this point; compare line 170.

         "A" super "R." The letters probably were meant to stand for "Anna" and "Ricardus," though other explanations are possible. On King Richard's fondness for such

badges of livery (and the menace they might represent), see Strohm, *Hochon's Arrow*, pp. 65 and 182–84, and especially Bowers, "*Pearl* in Its Royal Setting," pp. 136–41.

95   *secta*. Compare line 80.

115   *cuntis*. Equivalent to *cunctis*. Similarly spelled forms occur again at lines 139 ("cunta"), 426 ("cunta"), 453 ("cuntis"), and 469 ("cuntis"), though a form spelled *cunct-* occurs too, at line 427 ("cuncti").

121   *re sit et Anna*. Later in the poem (see line 434 ff. and corresponding explanatory note), Maidstone develops the etymological meaning of the queen's Christian name (from a Hebrew term meaning "grace"), and the sense of this remark also seems to depend on this meaning: the hope expressed is that the queen may prove to be as gracious in the event as her name suggests she might or should be.

150   *reddere*. A noun, meaning "surrender."

155   *Sex quater*. I.e., the twenty-four aldermen.

166   *phalangis*. I.e., "falding cloths."

170   No pentameter follows to close the couplet begun here, with the implication that at least a line of Maidstone's writing has been lost at this point, too; compare line 93.

183   *Strata*. I.e., "street."

205   *ligios*. I.e., "lieges."

212   *Pergama*. The Trojan citadel, used here to stand for the physical city of London (*Nova Troia*) itself, as distinct from the citizens (*corpora*) and their wealth (*divicie*), as part of Maidstone's representation of the city as a type of Troy; compare line 11.

223   *imperatoria proles*. Her father was the late emperor Charles IV (1316–78), on whom see Wallace, *Chaucerian Polity*, pp. 357–61.

229   *deus huic dedit illam*. The quasi-scriptural remark appears to liken Richard and Anne to God's originally perfect human creations, Adam and Eve, though there is no specific parallel: compare Genesis 2:22: "et aedificavit Dominus Deus costam,

quam tulerat de homine, in mulierem et adduxit eam ad hominem" ["And the Lord God built the rib which he took from Adam into a woman: and brought her to Adam"], and Genesis 3:12: "Dixitque homo: mulier quam dedisti sociam mihi, ipsa dedit mihi de ligno et comedi" ["And Adam said: The woman, whom thou gavest me to be my companion, gave me of the tree, and I did eat"].

233–34   *presentat equm vobis, licet hoc minus equo / Extiterit donum.* The punning on n. *equs* ("horse") and adj. *equs* ("fair") (from Classical Latin *aequus*) is not possible to translate.

250   *Pheton.* I.e., Phaeton, the exemplary bad driver from Greco-Roman mythology: having begged his father Helios' permission to try driving the solar car, Phaeton lost control of it and was fatally struck down by Zeus before his incompetence could set the world on fire. The version of the story best known to someone like Maidstone may have been that of Ovid, *Metamorphoses* 2.1–328.

251   *Femina feminea sua dum sic femina nudat.* The pun depends on one or the other of the occurrences of *femina* in this line being construed as a nominative/accusative plural form of the neuter noun *femor, -inis* ("thighs"), the root syllable of which is short by nature, unlike the first syllable of *femina, -ae*, which is long by nature; the problem is that Maidstone's line requires both of its occurrences of *femina* to have a long first syllable.

264   *Forum.* I.e., Cheapside.

269   *Bachum.* I.e., Bacchus. *Tetis*: I.e., Tethys, a titan, wife of Oceanus and mother of the sea-nymphs and river-spirits. The terms are used metonymically for "wine" and "water" respectively.

289   *ciphum.* Equivalent to a form of *scyphus* ("communion cup") in medieval usage.

293   *Materiam superavit opus.* Ovid, *Metamorphoses* 2.5: "materiam superabat opus."

314   *Obsequiis animos se quietasse suos.* The translation reflects a strict construction of the grammar; *suos* might instead be construed as referring to the king and queen.

320   *Angelici prefert ordinis effigiem.* Though the remark is biblical in some sense, there appears to be no particular close verbal parallel.

325–26   The uncharacteristic *ĕtas* (though see Appendix 4.4 for comparable occurrences) combines with the opacity of the phrase *Extat ut est maior, sedibus inferior* (none of the other accounts of the entry describes this part of the show at all instructively) to suggest that some corruption may afflict this couplet.

337–40   In this list too, Maidstone prefers ancient vocabulary (*fistula, tibia, timpana, lira,* etc.) to medieval terms that might have had more descriptive accuracy.

345   *episcopus urbis.* Robert Braybroke, bishop of London 1381–1404, a promoter of the cult of St. Erkenwald (compare line 348: "Erkenwaldi sancta sepulcra"). See Emden, *Biographical Register of the University of Oxford* 1.254–55.

351   *in Lud quoque porta.* The legend of Lud's construction of the city walls (and the derivation of the city's name from his) is recounted in Geoffrey of Monmouth, *The History of the Kings of Britain* 3.20 (also 1.17), trans. Thorpe, pp. 106 and 74; compare lines 479–80, below.

361–68   For the tradition that such catalogues of trees and beasts represent, see Curtius, *European Literature and the Latin Middle Ages*, especially pp. 194–95.

372   *Agnus et ecce dei.* John 1:29 "Altera die vidit Johannes Jesum venientem ad se, et ait: Ecce Agnus Dei, ecce qui tollit peccatum mundi" ["The next day, John saw Jesus coming to him; and he saith: Behold the Lamb of God. Behold him who taketh away the sin of the world"].

373   *quia.* Illogical, strictly, and so possibly corrupt.

397–98   *Ricardi quod fuit ante / Nomen.* I.e., Richard the Lion-hearted. On the accretion of quasi-legendary materials about this historical figure, see the still fundamental work of Paris, "Le roman de Richard Coeur de Lion," especially pp. 387–93, on the later fourteenth-century developments most nearly contemporary with Maidstone's writing. See also Broughton, *The Legends of King Richard I, Coeur de Lion.*

417   *Rex et apum caret omnis acu.* The notion would derive ultimately from the ancient science mentioned by the elder Pliny, *Historia naturalis* 11.17.52–53, though it would have become widely diffused in subsequent popular lore. Compare Thomas Hoccleve, *The Regiment of Princes*, lines 3375–81, where Hoccleve is probably drawing on some version of the *Ludus scaccorum.*

434   *gracia.* The (Hebrew) etymology was widely known; compare Bokenham, *Legends of Holy Women*, line 1498 ("Anne is as myche to seyn as 'grace'"), p. 41, or the Trinity College stanzaic *Life of Saint Anne*, line 211 ("The name of Anne to say hyt ys but grace"), in Parker, ed., *The Middle English Stanzaic Versions of the Life of Saint Anne*, p. 96. Forms of the term then recur throughout the rest of Maidstone's account of this exchange between queen and warden; for example, lines 436 ("Gracia"), 439 ("Grata"), and 451 ("grates").

439–44   Compare Esther, especially 7:3, "Ad quem illa respondit: Si inveni gratiam in oculis tuis, o rex, et si tibi placet, dona mihi animam meam, pro qua rogo, et populum meum pro quo obsecro" ["Then she answered: If I have found favour in thy sight, O king, and if it please thee, give me my life for which I ask, and my people for which I request"], and 8:5.

442   *Irritat edicta.* The verb is *Irrĭtat* ("invalidates") not *irrītat*, requiring the MS lection *edicta*, not *dicta*, as read by both Wright and Smith.

448   *virum.* I.e., "husband," Richard II.

454   *Westquemonasterium.* Equivalent to *Westmonasteriumque.* Compare Thomas Elmham, "On the Death of Henry IV," ed. Wright, *Political Poems and Songs* 2.122: "In Bethlem camera Westquemonasterio," also a pentameter line.

472   *tibi.* The shift of the queen's petition after this point, from such a singular form to the more formal second person plural (e.g., line 477 "velitis"), is not possible to translate.

479–80   The legends of Brutus and Arthur here alluded to also derive ultimately from Geoffrey of Monmouth, *The History of the Kings of Britain* 1.3–1.18 and 8.19–11.2 respectively, trans. Thorpe, pp. 54–74 and 204–61; compare line 351.

481   *regi . . . morituro.* I.e., with the exception of the Christ-King.

522   *didicere.* A preferable reading might be *docuere* ("taught").

Textual Notes

In addition to the manuscript's headings and marginalia, this apparatus lists departures from the manuscript, enclosed in brackets [ ] in the edited text, excepting the marks of punctuation, which are editorial, and the expansion of manuscript abbreviations, which are supplied passively throughout the text. The apparatus also lists the substantive variants (i.e., neither the orthographical variants nor the typographical errors) of the editions of Wright = **W** (distinguishing Wright 1838 = **Wa**, and Wright 1859 = **Wb** as necessary) and Smith = **S**.

Interlinear heading (before line 1): *Incipit concordia facta inter regem et civitatem Londonie.*

8   *sentis.* W: *senties (fortasse recte).*

Interlinear heading (before line 45): *Hic preparat se civitas in occursum regis.*

79   *H[o]s.* MS: *Hoos*; compare line 177.

80   *quemque.* W: *quaeque.*

87   *archifices.* W: *artifices.*

88   *lorimarius.* W: *lorinarius.*

89   *[Hic].* MS: *Ibi*; correction inserted in the margin.

92   *avigerulus.* W: *anigerulus.*

94   *bursistaque.* MS: *-que* is inserted above the line.

101   *quater.* W: *quatuor.*

Interlinear heading (before line 102): *Hic occurrunt cives regi.*

Interlinear heading (before line 130): *Hic reddit se civitas domino regi.*

Interlinear heading (before line 154): *Hic veniunt cives ad reginam.*

Interlinear heading (before line 160): *Hic tendit rex cum tota cohorte versus urbem.*

170   *ille.* W: *iste.*

176   *servet.* W: *servat.*

Interlinear heading (before line 177): *De pluvia que tunc accidit.*

177   *T[u]nc.* MS: *Tuunc*; compare line 79.

179   *pluerat.* W: *pluebat.*

Interlinear heading (before line 183): *De venia data exuli in Southwerk.*

190   *tribuit.* W: *tribuat.*

Interlinear heading (before line 191): *Hic fuit regina coronata.*

Interlinear heading (before line 197): *Hic presentat civitas regi duos dextrarios per cus-todem.*

209   *[est].* Omitted in MS.

Interlinear heading (before line 221): *Hic presentant regine palefridum.*

235   *leviter.* W: *leniter.*

241   *illa.* W: *iam.*

Interlinear heading (before line 225): *Hic progreditur rex cum tota cohorte versus Chepe.*

Marginal notation (next to lines 250–52): *de curru dominarum qui cecidit super pontem.*

253   *ille.* W: *iste.*

Marginal notation (next to lines 258–60): *de ornatu Chepe et aliarum platearum.*

260   *decus.* W: *pecus.*

Interlinear heading (before line 269): *Quomodo aqueductus dedit vinum et de ornatu eius.*

270   *ille.* W: *iste.*

271   *quasi.* W omits.

Interlinear heading (before line 275): *De turri mirabili in medio Chepe.*

276   *Cernit.* Corrected from *Cernunt* in MS.

287   *pendent.* W: *pendunt.*

294   *nova.* Wa: *novo.*

296   *el[o]quendo.* MS: *elequendo.*

Interlinear heading (before line 297): *Hic offert custos coronas regi et regine.*

303   *sensu.* W: *sensum.*
          omni. W: *omne.*

Marginal notation (next to lines 310–11): *hic riserunt parum rex et regina.*

312   *ei.* Wb: *eis.*

Interlinear heading (before line 317): *De ornatu secundi aqueductus ad portam Pauli.*

323   *micant.* W: *micat.*

330   *celicas ille sedet.* S: *ille sedet celicas.*

333   *oculus . . . auris.* W: *oculos . . . aures.*

Marginal notation (next to lines 335–36): *de instrumentis organicis.*

339   *Zambuce.* W: *Zambuca.*

Interlinear heading (before line 343): *Hic intravit rex monasterium sancti Pauli equis relictis.*

345   *O[c]currunt.* MS: *Orcurrunt.*

347   *Concomitantur.* W: *Concomitatur.*

Marginal notation (next to lines 351–53): *De ornatu porte Lud.*

355   *hiique.* W: *hii quoque.*

Interlinear heading (before line 357): *De deserto et Iohanne Baptista ad Barram Templi.*

Marginal notation (next to lines 361–62): *De arboribus diversis.*

364   *Ulm[u]s.* MS: *Ulms.*

Marginal notation (next to lines 365–66): *de diversitate bestiarum.*

Interlinear heading (before line 379): *Hic dantur regi et regine due tabule preciose cum ymaginibus.*

Interlinear heading (before line 393): *De verbis custodis ad regem in dando tabulas.*

407   *[u]t*. MS: *et*.

412   *velit*. W: *vellet*.

416   *tamen*. W: *tantum*.

Interlinear heading (before line 421): *Hic tetigit rex tabulas aureas sibi datas.*

Interlinear heading (before line 429): *Hic dantur tabule domine regine eiusdem figure.*

435   *nam*. W: *num*.

442   *edicta*. W, S: *dicta*.

Interlinear heading (before line 453): *Hic progreditur rex versus Westmonasterium et cives sequntur.*

458   *Tam*. W: *Iam*.

Interlinear heading (before line 463): *Quomodo regina corruit ante regem pro civibus.*

Interlinear heading (before line 467): *Supplicacio regine pro eisdem civibus.*

467   *mi*. S: *me*.

Interlinear heading (before line 493): *Responsio domini regis ad reginam.*

Interlinear heading (before line 499): *Hic alloquitur rex cives et reddit libertates.*

527   *Sit*. W: *Sic*.

Interlinear heading (before line 539): *Congratulacio civium pro restitutione libertatum et recessus eorum.*

Postlinear notation (after line 546): *Explicit concordia facta inter regem Riccardum secundum post conquestum et cives Londonie per fratrem Riccardum Maydiston Carmelitam sacre theologie doctorem anno domini millesimo CCC. nonagessima tertio.*

Appendix 1

Other Accounts of the 1392 Royal Entry

1.1 French epistolary report of 1392 (excerpt), ed. Helen Suggett, "A Letter Describing Richard II's Reconciliation with the City of London, 1392," *English Historical Review* 62 (1947), 212–13. The punctuation here below is editorial.

Et tantost come le Roy feust un poy passez Wandesworthe, le gardeyn de la ville ové lez aldermen encountrerent ovesque le Roy au pee. Le gardeyn porta en sa mayn un espé, et le pomel en haut et la point en sa mayn, et lez clyeffs de la ville, et qant ills furent devant le Roy, le gardeyn disoyt, genulant luy et sez compaignons, "Mon seignur liege, si sont voz lieges, qe se mettent en vostre grace et mercy lour vies et corps et toutz lour bienz, en requirant vostre grace et mercy." Et lour fuist dit depar le Roy q'ills dussent venir au paloys de Westmoster et la averoient lour response. Et le Roy fist Percy prendre l'espé et lez clyeffs et porter ovesqe luy, et puys le Roy chivacha avant. Et bien la, tret d'un arc, le Roy trova lez mesters de la ville, vestutz d'une suyte, chescun pur luy mesmes, et feuront arayés au chival de chescun part de chemyn, demorantz trestoutz en lour placez tanqe le Roy fuist passez toutz, et duré le montaigne par deshors Wandesworthe entour une lewe. Et qant le Roy fuist passé toutz, il chivacha au part de chimyn et lessa toutz les gentz de la ville passez avant, et puys chivacha luy mesmes avant apres eux en mesme la compaignye. Et qant il fuist pluis pres de la ville, il fuist encontré ové toutz lez religiouses, freres, moygnez, prestrez, clercz, et enfantz, chantantz auscuns "Te Deum laudamus" et auscuns "Summe Trinitati." Et a sa entré a la pont, le gardeyn et lez aldermen luy presenteront de deux grandez coursers, trappés de drap d'or, partiz blanc et rouge, et une grande paleffray a la Roigne, trappéz de mesme la suyte. Et a sa venue en Chepe, parentre lez deux croys, vendront deux angeles, hors d'une nuwe, l'une apportant une corone pur le Roy, et le gardeyn le prist et le presenta au Roy, et un altre corone et a la Roigne. Et a Poules, la procession de l'esglise luy encontra, et le Roy descendy et ala en l'esglise et offrist. Et puis chivacha avant, et a Ludgate le gardeyn et lez aldermen presenteront le Roy d'une beale table d'or pur alter, et la Roigne d'une altre. Et bien entour Savoye, lez gentz de ville demoroient et lessent le Roy passer, et a Westmoster la procession luy encontra, et il s'en ala en le paloys et se vesti en une longe gowne, qar il avoit chivachez tout jour court. Et puis s'en ala en la sale et s'asist en une see en haut, qe fuist fait devant le grant see, arrayez dez draps d'or, et tretoutz le sale penduz de aras, et tretoutz lez comunes feurent devant luy. Et adonqe vient la Roigne et l'erchevesqe d'une part, et l'evesqe de Londrez d'altre part et eux mistrent as genoiles devant le Roy, luy priantz de prendre sez lieges en sa grace et mercy. Et puis fuist dit depar le Roy, par la bouche de seneschal, qe le Roy avoit esté poisant qe sicome Londres estoit sa chambre q'il avoit esté si malement gardés, et plusours altrez paroles queux je ne say escrire. Mays l'effect fuist qe le Roy lez prist en sa grace et lez granta toutz lour franchisez, si franchement come ills unqes avoient, forspris deux ou troys, qe lour dussent estre mostrez et moderez par son grant conseil. Et puis mangea les espyces et le vyn be[v]oit, et chescun s'en ala, et le Roy s'en ala a Kenyngton' a souper. Et lendemayn mangea en la ville ovesqe le gardeyn et le Roynge auxi, et la feust presentez au Roy une grande table d'argent et enamailez, et feust assez grant pur le reredors d'un alter, et a ma dame la Roigne une hanap de beryle et une ewer herneisez d'or. Et apres lour departir vers Westmostier, certeynz mesters de la ville feuront arrayés dez grandez vessellz, de shoutez et barges bien apparailez, et entre eux lez gentz de mester daunsantz et fesantz grant menstracye, et aleront ovesqe le Roy jesqe Westmostier. Et en alant par le chymyn, ills fesoyent le Roy et la Roigne boire ovesqe eux. Et apres ceo, le Roy fist toutz lez gentz de mester de venir ovesqe luy en son paloys, et illeoqes f[i]st tretoutz boire, et puys departiront ovesqe tresgrand joye et solas. Et, qant a plusours altrez affaires qe feuront ordeignés en la Citee, ne vous say certefyer, come dez conduitz de la ville, qe feurent diversement apparailez, currantz vyn et appareylez ovesqe diversez peynturez et ymageryes, et angels fesantz grant melodie et menstralcie, et ensi en plusours partyes de la ville, et lez rues apparaylez dez drapz, en auscun lieu, d'or et de soy. Et le offre fuist de cent mille liverez. Et le Roy lez ad pardoné, forsqe ditz mille liveres queux il avera en mayn et sez diz anz apres chescun an deux mille marcz.

[As soon as the king was a little past Wandsworth, the warden of the city and the aldermen met him, on foot. The warden carried a sword in his hand, the pommel up and the point in his hand, and the keys to the city; and when they were before the king, the warden spoke, him and his companions on their knees: "My liege lord, those of us here, who submit themselves — their beings and bodies, and all their belongings — to your grace and mercy, we are your lieges, beseeching your grace and mercy." And it was announced to them on the king's behalf that they should come to Westminster Palace and there they should have their answer. The king caused Percy to receive the sword and the keys and to carry them with him, and then the king rode on. Near by, the length of a bow-shot, the king came upon the guilds of the city, each by itself, dressed in distinctive livery; they were drawn up on horseback all along the road, remaining each in their places until the king had passed them all in review, the demonstration lasting from beyond Wandsworth for a considerable space. When the king had passed all in review, he rode to the side on the road and let all the people of the city pass before him, and then he himself rode on after them, keeping to their companies. And when he came nearer the city, he was met by all the religious of the city — friars, monks, priests, clerks, and boys, some singing the *Te Deum* and some the *Summe Trinitati*. Upon his entry onto the bridge, the warden and aldermen presented him with two great coursers, trapped with cloth of gold, parti-colored white and red, and a great palfrey for the queen, trapped in the same manner. At his entry into Cheapside, between the two crosses, came two angels down from a cloud, the one bearing a crown for the king, which the warden took and presented to the king, and the other another crown, which was presented to the queen. Then, at Paul's, a procession from the church came out to meet him, and the king dismounted, went into the church, and made offering. Then he rode on, and at Ludgate the warden and aldermen presented the king with a beautiful altarpiece of pure gold, and the queen with another. Near the Savoy, the people of the city waited, to let the king process past them, and from Westminster a procession came out to meet him, and he went into the palace and dressed himself in a long gown, for he had been riding the whole day long. Then he entered his hall and seated himself on a high throne, set up in front of the great throne and decorated with cloth of gold; throughout the hall hung arras, and throughout it the commons stood before him. Then came the queen and the archbishop from one side, and the bishop of London from the other. They betook themselves before the king on bended knee, beseeching him to receive his lieges into his grace and mercy. Then it was pronounced on behalf of the king, by the voice of his chamberlain, that the king was mindful that it had been his own dwelling place, London itself, that had so mistreated him — with numerous other remarks that I do not know how to record; but the import was that the king was taking them into his grace and granted them all their liberties, as liberally as they had ever been, excepting two or three, which required to be scrutinized and amended for them by his great council. Then he took spices and drank wine, and all departed, and the king betook himself to Kennington for supper. The next day he dined in the city with the warden, as did also the queen; and there was presented to the king a great table of silver gilt and enameling — it was great enough for the reredos of an altar — and to my lady the queen a beryl hanaper and a ewer encased in gold. After their leaving for Westminster, certain city guilds were arrayed thereabouts, with great vessels and decorated barges cabled together; on them the guildsmen danced and made merry, and went with the king all the way to Westminster. As they went along the way, they caused the king and queen to drink with them. Afterwards, the king caused all the guildsmen to come with him into the palace, where he caused all to drink, whence they departed in great comfort and joy. As for the many other matters that were arranged in the city, I cannot know how to explain: the conduits of the city, which were variously decorated, ran with wine and were decorated with diverse paintings and imageries, and angels made great melody and minstrelsy; in several parts of the city, the streets were hung with draperies, in each quarter, of cloth of gold and of silk. A hundred thousand pounds was offered him. But the king forgave them it, excepting ten thousand pounds, which he took in hand immediately, and two thousand marks to be given him annually in each of the subsequent ten years.]

1.2 *The Westminster Chronicle 1381–1394*, ed. and trans. L. C. Hector and Barbara F. Harvey (Oxford: Clarendon Press, 1982), pp. 502–07.

Demum mediantibus amicis pro eis et precipue domina regina Anglie, que iteratis vicibus, immo multociens, prostravit se ad pedes domini regis tam ibi quam aput Notyngham, obnixe et sedule deprecando pro dicta civitate London' et pro statu civium ejusdem quatinus ut ipse suam indignacionem ab eis averteret ne tam celebris civitas cum tam numerosa plebe in ea degente pereat inconsulte, scilicet calore iracundie emulorum suorum, ad hec clemens et benignus rex pietate motus ad instanciam domine regine aliorumque suorum procerum et magnatum remisit eis omnia que in eum deliquerunt sub ista condicione, quod infra decem annos proximo sequentes solvant ei aut ejus certis attornatis quadraginta milia librarum, et hoc ad verum valorem, videlicet in jocalibus aut in pecunia numerata, et quod venirent erga eum et exciperent eum aput Wandlesworthe decenti apparatu, unaquaque ars dicte civitatis in secta sua et in equis, et per medium dicte civitatis honorifice perducerent eum usque Westmon' die ad hoc prefixo, qui fuit xxj. mensis Augusti. Londonienses vero consenserunt ista premissa pro eorum modulo percomplere ac in omnibus pro posse votis regiis obedire. Quid ultra? Venit dies prefixus; rex de manerio suo de Shene in regio apparatu iter suum sumpsit versus London'; erga quem exierunt Londonienses ex omnibus artibus civitatis ejusdem, equestres omnes, usque Wandleworth' et quelibet ars in propria sua secta; qui pre multitudine a ponte London' protendebantur ultra villam de Kenyngeton', et annumerantur ad xxij. milia equitum: erat quoque numerus peditum infinitus. In primo namque occursu aput Wandelesworth' optulerunt domini regi Londonienses gladium et claves civitatis predicte, deinde ad portam pontis London' presentarunt domino regi duos equos electos vocatos courceres: unus illorum erat albi coloris et alter rubei coloris, cum sellis argenteis ac splendide deauratis; ibi eciam dederunt domine regine unum pulchrum palefridum cum sella aurea adornatum. Erat autem pons London' et cetere strate eminenciores dicte civitatis diversorum pannorum aureorum, sericorum aliorumque bistinctorum lucide perornate. Procedebat ulterius, venit in Stratam

Piscariam, ubi venerunt duo juvenes preclari forma decori specie cum duobus thuribulis aureis thurificantes eum honorifice, prout decebat. Et processit parumper, venit in vicum qui vocatur Chepe; ibi de quadam alta structura descenderunt quasi duo angeli in specie puerorum, ut erant, quendam cantum egregie et suaviter modulantes ac in eorum manibus duas aureas coronas habentes magni valoris: primus vero coronam quam in manu sua gestabat posuit super caput regis; alter quoque coronam quam ipse gerebat imposuit capiti regine. Sicque abhinc lento passu coronati venerunt ad Temple Barre, ubi presentarunt sibi unam tabulam auream valentem centum marcas. Abhinc recto tramite perrexerunt usque ad portam monasterii Westm', ubi occurrebat ei prior et conventus revestiti et albis capis induti cum crucibus, cereis, thuribulis, et textibus: quos videns rex et regina ilico descenderunt de equis et depositis coronis osculati sunt textus. Deinde in revertendo versus ecclesiam, conventus cantabat responsorium "Agnus in altari"; demum venientes ante magnum altare conventus cantebat antiphonum "Solve jubente". Dominus rex interim super gradus marmareos devote genuflexit et post ipsum venit regina et similes devociones peregit. Dicta collecta pro rege conventus intrabat ad feretrum Sancti Edwardi cum illa antiphona "Ave, Sancte rex Edwarde". Completa oracione ac factis suis oblacionibus rex in suum palacium est reversus.

Mox Baldewynus de Radyngton' custos London' ex parte Londoniensium invitavit dominum regem ad prandium erga diem crastinum. Annuit rex: convivio celebrato Londonienses optulerunt domino regi unam tabulam mensalem argenteam ac deauratam longitudine novem pedum, valentem quingentas marcas. Istis sic decursis, quadam die non longe postea in magna aula Westmon' sedens rex in sua sede regia concessit prefatis Londoniensibus omnes libertates quas ab eis abstulerat exceptis tribus. . . .

[At length through the intercession, on behalf of the Londoners, of friends, conspicuous among them the queen (who more than once, indeed on many occasions, both at Windsor and at Nottingham, prostrated herself at the king's feet in earnest and tireless entreaty for the city and the welfare of its citizens that he would cease to direct his anger against them and would not let so famous a city and its teeming masses perish without due consideration simply because of the burning passion of its enemies), the king's mild and kindly nature was moved by pity, and persuaded by the queen and others among his nobles and prominent men he forgave the Londoners all their offences against him on condition that within the next ten years they paid him or his unquestionable attorneys £40,000 in real terms of jewels or specie, and that on the day appointed for his progress, which was 21 August, they should come out to meet him and receive him at Wandsworth with appropriate pomp, each city craft in its own livery and mounted on horseback, to escort him with all honor through the city to Westminster. The Londoners agreed to carry out these conditions to the letter, so far as they could, and to comply in all respects to the best of their ability with the king's wishes. What is there to add? The appointed day came; the king set out in royal splendour from his manor of Sheen on the road to London; to meet him representatives of every craft in the City, all mounted, came out as far as Wandsworth, each craft in its own livery; the throng was so great that it stretched from London Bridge beyond Kennington, mustering 22,000 horsemen and an uncountable number on foot. At the first encounter at Wandsworth the Londoners handed to the king a sword and the keys of the city; at the gate of London Bridge they presented him with two carefully chosen horses of the kind called "coursers," one white and the other a bay, with saddles of silver magnificently gilded: and here also they gave to the queen a beautiful palfrey adorned by a gold saddle. London Bridge itself and the chief city streets were gaily decorated with [banners of] assorted cloths of gold, silks, and other double-dyed fabrics. The king went on his way, and when he reached Fish Street there appeared two young men of fine figure and handsome appearance carrying two gold thuribles with which, as was fitting, they did him honour by censing him. A little further on he came to the street known as Eastcheap, and here there descended from a lofty structure two "angels" in the shape of boys (which is what they were) caroling a melody with singular art and sweetness and having in their hands two gold crowns of great costliness: the first boy placed on the king's head the crown he was carrying in his hand, and the crown borne by the other was set by him on the head of the queen. And so, wearing their crowns, they went from there at a stately pace to Temple Bar, where they were presented with a gold table worth 100 marks before proceeding by the direct route to the gate of the monastery at Westminster. Here the king was met by the prior and convent in new clothes and wearing white copes, with crosses, candles, censers, and Gospels: on seeing them the king and queen at once dismounted and, laying aside their crowns, kissed the Gospels. On the way back to the church the convent sang the responsory "Agnus in altari" and upon their eventual arrival before the high altar the antiphon "Solve jubente." Meanwhile the king knelt reverently on the marble steps and after him came the queen and performed similar devotions. When the collect for the king had been said, the convent went into St. Edward's shrine to the accompaniment of the antiphon "Ave, Sancte Rex Edwarde." When he had finished his prayers and made his offerings, the king returned to his palace.

Soon afterwards Baldwin Raddington, the warden of London, invited the king on behalf of the Londoners to a banquet on the following day. The king accepted: and when the banquet was held the Londoners presented to the king a silver and gilt table nine feet long and worth 500 marks. One day, shortly after these events had run their course, the king took his seat on the royal throne in the great hall at Westminster and granted to the Londoners all the privileges he had withdrawn from them, with three exceptions.]

1.3. *Knighton's Chronicle 1337–1396*, ed. and trans. G. H. Martin (Oxford: Clarendon Press, 1995), pp. 546–48.

Interea, Dominica proxima post festum Assumpcionis Beate Marie, omnes potenciores ciuitatis uenerunt ad regem, et submiserunt se et omnia bona sua regi, et tunc primo recepit eos in suam graciam.

Die uero Mercurii sequenti, rex disposuit se uenire Londonias. Et occurrerunt ei ciues equestres, multitudine quasi innumerabili, et qui non habebant equos dederunt ei obuiam pedestres. Mulieres quoque et infantes se ei monstrauerunt. Episcopus quoque Londoniensis, cum cetu cleri tocius ciuitatis, nullo ordine uel gradu, aut condicione uel sexu, ecclesiastice dignitatis excusato, cum ingenti honoris tripudio et regi et regine processit obuiam. Fertur in illa processione plusquam quingentos pueri in superpelliciis extitisse.

Insuper et ciues ornauerunt facies domorum et camerarum suarum per omnes uicos, plateas, et stratas quo rex et regina transituri erant, a Sancto Georgio usque ad Westmonasterium. Saltem in dignioribus edificiis, uestibus cultioribus aureis et argenteis ueluetis syndonicis sicladibus, aliisque preciosis prout possibilitas cuiuscumque attingere poterat ut ubique, aqueductu in Chepa uinum rubeum et album affluenter emanante, puero quoque in uestibus albis in forma angeli cum cupa aurea desuper stante, et uinum regi et regine ad bibendum offerente.

Interea offerunt regi unam coronam auream magni precii, et alteram coronam auream regine. Et post pusillum procedentes, conferunt regi unam tabulam auream de Trinitate, ad precium octingentarum librarum, similiter et regine aliam tabulam auream, de Sancta Anna, quam ipsa in speciali deuocione habebat, eo quod ipsamet Anna uocabatur. Et tantos ac tales honores et mirabiles regi impenderunt, quales nulli alii regi et huius regni retroactis temporibus meminimus impensos fuisse.

Sicque progredientes, perduxerunt regem et reginam in aulam Westmonasteriensem. Rege uero sedente in sede regali, et omni populo coram eo stante, quidam ex ore regis regraciabatur populo de innumerositate magnifici honoris, et immense munificencie, ab eis regi impensa, et quo ad sua negocia incumbencia, in proximo parliamento se debere habere finale responsum.

[Meanwhile, on the Sunday after the Assumption of the Blessed Virgin (18 Aug. 1392) all the greater men of the city came before the king, and submitted their persons and all their possessions to the king, and he then for the first time took them back into his grace.

Then, upon the following Wednesday (21 Aug. 1392) the king arranged to go to London, and the citizens came to him in a company as it were beyond number, mounted, and those who had no horses came out to meet him on foot, and the women and children showed themselves to him. The bishop of London also, with all the clergy of the city, none of any order, grade, condition, or sex of the church's dignity being excused, came with the most auspicious honour, and processed before the king and the queen. It was reported that the procession included more than 500 children clad in surplices.

And the citizens also decorated the fronts of their houses and chambers along all the roads, places, and streets by which the king and queen passed from St. George's to Westminster, at least on the more important buildings, with splendid hangings, of gold and silver, velvet, muslin cloth, and other costly things everywhere, all of the best that each of them could contrive, and there was white and red wine flowing from the conduit in Cheapside, and a boy dressed as an angel in white robes, with a golden cup, offering the king and queen wine to drink.

And amongst other things they offered the king a golden crown of great price, and another golden crown to the queen, and a little further on they gave the king a golden tablet depicting the Trinity, which cost £800. And the queen had another tablet, with St. Anne, whom she held in special devotion, because she herself was called Anne. And so many and such honours and marvels were lavished upon the king that no other king of this realm in past times can be remembered to have enjoyed the like.

And thus they went on their way, and led the king and queen into the Westminster Hall. And there with the king sitting upon the throne and all the people standing before him, they heard from the king's own mouth his thanks for the incalculably splendid honours and great munificence that they had shown him. And as for the matters perpending, they should have a final answer in the next parliament.]

1.4 1377–1419 *Brut* continuation (see above, p. 19n65), ed. Friedrich W. D. Brie, *The Brut, or, The Chronicles of England*, EETS o.s. 131 and 136 (London: Kegan Paul, Trench, Trübner, and Co., Ltd., 1906–08), 2.347–48.

And þan þe King with-ynne ij dayeȝ aftir, com to London; and þe Maire of London, schereueȝ, aldremen, and alle þe worthi cite aftirward, redyn ayens þe King yn gode araye vnto þe heth on þis syde þe maner of Schene, submittyng humyly hem self, and mekely, with almaner of obeysaunceȝ vn-to hym, as þay owed to do. And þus þai brouȝt þe King and þe Quene to London. And whanne þe King come to þe gate of þe Brygge of London, þere þay presentid hym with a mylke-white stede, sadelled and brydilled, & trapped with white cloth of golde and red parted togadir, and þe Quene a palfraye alle white, trappid yn þe same aray with white and rede, and þe condite3 of London [r]onnen white wyne and rede, for al maner pepill to drynke of. And betuene Seint Poule3 and the Cros yn Chepe, þere was made a stage, a ryalle, stondyng vpon hygh; a[n]d þerynne were mony angelis, with dyuers melodie3 and songe; and an aungell come doun fro þe stage on high, by a vice, and sette a croune of golde & precious stone3 & perles apon þe Kinge3 hed, and anoþer on the Quene3 hed; and so the citezenys brought þe King and þe Quene vnto Westmynstre, yn-to his palice at Westmynstre, & presentyd hym with ij basyns of syluyr, & ovirgilte, fulle of coyned golde, the summa of xx m^t li, prayng hym, of his mercy and lordschip and specialle grace, þat þay my3t have his gode loue, and libertee3 and Fraunche3es like as þay hadde before tyme3, and by his lettre3 patente3 confermed. And þe Quene, and oþer worthi lorde3 & ladie3, ffillyn on hir kneys, and besou3t the King of grace to conferme þis. Thanne þe King toke vp þe Quene, and grauntyd hir alle hir askyng, and þanne þei þanked þe King and þe Quene and went home ayene.

1.5. Thomas Walsingham, *Thomae Walsingham, quondam monachi S. Albani, historia anglicana*, ed. Henry Thomas Riley, Rolls Series 28.1, 2 vols. (London: Longman, Green, Longman, Roberts, and Green, 1863–64), 2.210–11.

Cumque et cives regressi fuissent, et proceres qui cum Rege fuerant, et reliquus populus, ad propria remeassent, Rex audiens Londonienses in tristitia constitutos et mente lapsos, ait suis; — "Vadam," inquit, "Londonias, et consolabor cives; nec patiar eos ultra de mea gratia desperare." Quæ sententia, mox ut cognita fuit in civitate, incredibili jocunditate replevit omnes; unde omnes et singuli ei generaliter statuerunt occurrere, et non minores expensas facere in exenniis et donativis quam fecerant in ejus Coronatione. Rex igitur, ut venit Londonias, tanta gloria, tanta pompa, tanta varietate diversorum apparatuum, est susceptus, quanta suscipi decuisset aliquem regem triumphantem. Nam equos et phaleras, tabulas aureas et argenteas, pannos aureos et holosericos, pelves et lavatoria de fulvo metallo, aurum in pecunia, gemmas et monilia, tam ditia, tam nobilia, tam speciosa, donaverunt eidem, ut cunctorum valor, et pretium, non posset facile æstimari.

[When the citizens had departed, and the nobles who had been with the king and the rest had returned to their homes, the king, hearing that the Londoners were remorseful and downcast, spoke to his servants and said, "I will go to London and will console the citizens, nor will I allow them any longer to despair of my grace." As soon as this sentiment had been made known in the city, it filled all with unbelievable joy; whence all and sundry determined to go out in a body to meet him and to spend no less on presents and gifts than they had for his coronation. Consequently, when the king came to London, he was received with such glory, such pomp, and such a wealth of diverse devices, as would have been fitting for receiving a ruler come in triumph. For they presented him with horses and horse-trappings, gilt and silver tablets, cloth of gold and hanging silks, basins and ewers of the tawny metal, coined gold, gemstones and jewelry, so costly, so noble, and so rich, that the value and price of the things cannot easily be counted.]

Appendix 2

Accounts of Richard's 1377 Coronation Entry

2.1 *Chronicon Angliae, ab anno domini 1328 usque ad annum 1388, auctore monacho quodam Sancti Albani*, ed. Edward Maunde Thompson, Rolls Series 64 (London: Longman, and Co., 1874), pp. 153–56.

Die præcedente diem coronationis regiæ, magnates et plebs numerosa regni Londoniis confluxerant, ut supra taxavimus; et post horam nonam, proceres regni, cum Londoniensibus aliisque multis quos amor regis attraxerat, equis vecti sublimibus, ad Turrim, ubi pro tunc rex fuerat, properarunt. Dispositisque tunc ibidem qui præcederent et qui sequerentur, equitare cœperunt versus Westmonasterium per frequentissimos vicos civitatis. Quæ nimirum civitas tot pannis aureis et argenteis, tot holosericis, aliisque adinventionibus, quæ animos intuentium oblectarent, ornata fuerat, ut putares te ibidem vel Cæsarianos triumphos cernere, vel Romam, ut quondam fuerat, in præcellenti decore. Tantus itaque populus adventaverat, ut eos vici celeberrimi capere non valerent, sed, ut ita dicam,

— "Gradibus evectis ad culmina crucis
"Quamplures, avidique suum cognoscere regem,
"Edita murorum longa statione coronant."

Igitur in tanta equitatione præcessere cives Baiocenses, antecedentibus in una secta tibiis et tubis, et tympanis, aliisque exquisitis generibus musicorum. Hos sequebatur una de custodiis civitatis, quas wardas appellant, et ipsi in secta sua et maxima melodia. Quos sequebantur Alemanni regis stipendiarii, et ipsi aliis dissimiles in vestitu. Deinde secuta est et alia custodia civitatis, priori similis in apparatu; quam sequebantur Vasconenses, et ipsi vario superioribus habituum colore fulgentes. Mox etiam cives Londonienses, qui residui fuerant, secuti sunt Vasconenses equitatione longissima, ita ut numerarentur ex eis in una secta ad tria millia et septingentos. Hos sequebantur comites et barones regni, cum suis militibus et armigeris, in amictu similes regi suo. Nam indumenta omnium erant alba; qui color profecto regis innocentiam figurabat. Capitaneus de la Bewche, cum suis, inter regem et dominos in secta sua nobiliter equitabat. Tunc Angliæ marescallus, qui pro tunc fuerat dominus

101

Concordia facta inter regem et cives Londonie

Henricus Percy, et senescallus regni, videlicet dux Lancastriæ, cum militibus eisdem adjunctis, inequitantes equos nobiles et prægrandes, ut viam inter turbas regi facerent inoffensam, incedebant. De quibus mirum contigit, in hac equitatione adeo modeste se habuerunt, turbas tam modeste, tam facete, ut viæ cederent, monuerunt, ut nullum e tanta turba illo die, nec in crastino, verbo vel facto læderent quovismodo; unde contigit, ut pene totius vulgi favorem, quibus ante suspecti fuerant et odibiles, lucrarentur.

Rex autem, insidens magnum dextrarium, tantæ personæ aptum, stratumque regaliter, sequebatur illos. Cujus gladium, manibus elevatum, portabat ante eum dominus Symon Burle. Dominus quoque Nicholaus Bonde ejus frenum duxit, incedendo pedes. Regem vero sequebantur milites et coætanei sui, atque domus regiæ familiares. Nec defuit tantæ turbæ magna vis lituum et tubarum; nam turba seorsum suos tubicines præcedentes habebat, statutique fuerant per Londonienses super aquæductum, et super turrim in eodem foro, quæ in honorem regis facta fuerat, tubicines qui clangerent in adventu regis. Qui omnes simul juncti clangentes, sonum mirabilem audientibus reddiderunt. Fuit igitur dies ille dies jocunditatis et lætitiæ, dies, ut ita dicam, clangoris et buccinæ, dies diu exspectatus renovationis pacis et legum patriæ, quæ jam diu exsulaverant desidia regis senis et avaritia obsecundantium sibi servorum ejus.

Ad honorem insuper regium, cives ordinaverant ut per fistulæ aquæductus efflueret abundans vinum, et per totum tempus equitationis, id est, per tres et amplius horas, jugiter emanaret. Factum etiam fuerat quoddam castrum habens turres quatuor, in superiori parte fori venalium, quod Chepe nuncupatur; de quo etiam per duas partes vinum defluxit abundanter. In turribus autem ejus quatuor virgines speciosissimæ collocatæ fuerant, staturæ et ætatis regiæ, vestibus albis indutæ, in qualibet turri una; quæ adventanti regi procul aurea folia in ejus faciem efflaverunt, et propius accedenti, florenos aureos et sophisticos super eum et ejus dextrarium projecerunt. Cum autem ante castellum venisset, ciphos aureos acceperunt, et implentes eos vino ad fistulas dicti castelli, regi atque dominis obtulerunt. In summitate castelli, quæ ad modum tholi inter quatuor turres elevata fuerat, positus erat angelus aureus, tenens auream coronam in manibus, qui tali ingenio factus fuerat, ut adventanti regi coronam porrigeret inclinando. Adinventa sunt illo die in civitate et alia multa in honorem regis, quæ numerare per singula longum foret. Nam singuli per vicos et plateas decertarunt, quis ei propensiorem reverentiam exhiberet. Igitur cum tanto plebis civiumque tripudio, cum tanto dominorum procerumque favore perductus est ad palatium regium prope Monasterium Occidentale, ubi illa nocte quievit.

[The day before the day of the king's coronation, magnates and numerous commoners of the kingdom assembled at London, as was judged above; and after Nones (mid afternoon), the nobles of the realm, borne on lofty steeds, along with the Londoners and the many others whom love for the king drew to the place, thronged to the Tower, where the king stayed at that time. Having arranged who would lead and who would follow, they then began their ride thence towards Westminster, through the thronging streets of the city. The city proper was decked out with such a quantity of cloth of gold and of silver, such a quantity of silken banners and other devices, to fire the imaginations of onlookers, that you would have thought you saw there some Caesar's triumph, or even Rome itself, as it was of old, in all its exceeding glory. Such a gathering of people made its way there that even those great streets were not able to contain them all; instead, so to speak,

> "Thronging afoot to the hill of the cross,
>   So many longing to recognize
> Their king, they crown the walls in ranks."

In this great riding forth, the citizenry of Bayeux went in front, led by trumpets, horns, drums, and select other musicians, all in distinctive livery. After these there followed representatives from one of the administrative units of the city, which are called "wards," they too in distinctive livery and with much music. After them there followed the king's German mercenaries, these too vested differently from the rest. Next followed representatives from the rest of the wards of the city, like the earlier ones in their array, and Gascons followed them, resplendently dressed in colors different from the aforegoing. Next, following the Gascons, came what freemen of the city of London still remained, making a procession so sizable that, in a single liveried company among them, thirty-seven hundred could be counted. Then followed the counts and barons of the realm, with their knights and squires, in raiment like that of their king: the vestment of all of them was white, a color with which to represent the king's innocence. The captain of Calais and his retainers, in livery, rode nobly between king and lords. Then came on the marshall of England, being at that time the Lord Henry Percy, and the king's chamberlain, namely, the duke of Lancaster, with knights accompanying the same, riding tremendous great horses, in order to make way for the king safely to pass through the crowd. The wonder of it was that, throughout the procession, these two conducted themselves so gently, prayed the crowd to make way so gently and so kindly that, in the whole crowd, they affronted not a one, in any wise, by word or by deed, neither that day nor the next, the consequence being that they were rewarded with the good will of almost the whole of the populace, amongst whom they had been distrusted and hated before.

Then, astride a great charger, regally trapped, as befit so grand a personage, the king himself came on after them. Afore him, the Lord Simon Burley bore up his sword, holding it on high; likewise, the Lord Nicholas Bonde, going afoot, held his bridle; and there followed after the king peers of his own age, as well as the members of the royal household. Nor did a throng of such dimension want great might of trumpets and wind instruments, for the throng had with it its own horn-players going in front, and the Londoners had stationed bands of musicians — atop the conduits, and atop the towers that had been erected in the marketplace to honor the king — to herald the advent of the king. The lot of them together, all roaring at once, produced a sound that struck those hearing it with wonder. It was a day, that day, of merriment and of rejoicing, a day, so to speak, of fanfares and of trumpetry, a long-anticipated day, moreover, of the rebirth of peace and of the rule of law at home, a day which the old king's indolence and the rapacity of the servile types whom he had manipulating him had long put off.

Additionally to honor the king, the citizens had ordained that the spouts of the conduit should flow freely with wine, and that throughout the whole of the procession — for three hours or longer — it should pour forth constantly. There had been built a kind of castle, with four turrets, in the upper part of the public market, called the Cheap, from which wine flowed freely at two places. On its turrets were set four lovely maidens, clothed in white vestments, of the same size and age as the king, one on each turret. Upon the king's coming forth in the distance, they poured out gilt leaves at his appearance, and, when he drew nearer, they scattered likenesses of gilt florins over him and his mount. When he had come up to the castle, they took down golden cups, and, filling them with wine from the spouts of the said castle, they offered them to the king and the lords to drink. Upon the castle's pinnacle, which had been erected between the four turrets, in the manner of a belfry, had been set a golden angel, bearing a golden crown in its hands, which was constructed with such ingenuity that, upon the king's coming forth, bending down, it reached out the crown towards him. There were discovered that day in the city moreover numerous other devices, in honor of the king, which would take too long to enumerate singly here. For in every street and street corner, all strove to do him the more profound reverence. In such manner, with great rejoicing of the commons and freemen, and great favor of the lords and nobles, he was conveyed to the royal palace at Westminster, where he rested that night.]

2.2 *The Anonimalle Chronicle 1333 to 1381*, ed. V. H. Galbraith (Manchester: Manchester University Press, 1927; rpt. 1970), pp. 107–08.

A comensement le mequerdy avaunt la coronacione, apres la houre de noune, toutz les graundes seignurs queux furount presentz en la cite et le meir et les aldermen et les communes de Loundres chivacherent a le toure de Loundres ou le prince fuit et illeoqes attenderent avaunt le toure le avenw del prince. Et au darrein le dit prince veint de la toure en vesture de blaunk drape bien et honurablement arraye come affert a teil seignur et toutz ses chivalers en mesme la suyt et chivacherount devers Loundres. Et a comensement de lour chivache, chivacherent les communes de Loundres en vesture de blaunk et puis les esquiers des seignours et chivalers et puys chivalers et apres eux les aldermen et apres eux le meir et les deus viscountz toutez en vesture de blaunk et apres, le duk de Loncastre et les countz de Caumbrigge et de Herforth et adonqes le prince par luy mesmes par graunde espace et apres le prince les countz et barones et autres seignurs, et chivacherent parmy Loundres et parmy Chepe devers le palays de Wymoustre et en my lieu de Chepe une toure de canvays depaynte fuist, sutilment fait par suppowelle de merisme, en quel tour furount faitz quater torettes, en queux furount quater damosels tresbelles et bien arraies, et les ditez damosels getterent besauntz dore devers le prince; et enmy la dite toure fuist fait une petit clocher et amount le clocher fuist esteaunt une aungelle portaunt une corone dore et moustraunt al dit prince pur luy comforter. Mesme celle te[m]ps le cunditz en Chepe fuit depaynte de diverses colours et currust a ceste foitz de vine vermaille et blaunk, qe chescune qe vodroit, purroit en la chaloure boyr a volunte; et le dit vine fuist sawe par graundes cuves saunz perde en queux le vine decurrast. Et le dit prince chivacha par Fletstrett tanqe le palays de Wymoustre pur reposer et prendre sa ease et les autres seignurs retournerent a Loundres et aliours a lour hostelles.

[First of all, the Wednesday before the coronation, after Nones, all the great lords who were about the city, the mayor, aldermen, and commons of London, all rode out to the Tower of London, where the prince was staying, there before the Tower to attend upon the prince's entry. Thereafter, the said prince came out from the Tower, vested in white cloth, honorably well arrayed, as was fitting for a lord of such stature, as did all his knights, in the same array, and together they rode on towards London. At the head of the procession, there rode the London commons, vested in white, then the squires of the lords and knights, then the knights, and after them the aldermen, then after them the mayor and the two viscounts, all vested in white, and thereafter the duke of Lancaster and the earls of Cambridge and Hereford; then came the prince himself, considerably set apart; after the prince came the earls and barons and other lords; and they rode through London and through the Cheap towards the palace at Westminster. Set up in the middle of the Cheap stood a tower of painted canvas, curiously constructed, over timber support-beams; about the tower were four turrets, in which stood four damsels, exceedingly lovely and beautifully arrayed, and these said damsels threw gold coins in the direction of the prince's coming. Within the said tower had also been built a small belfry, and on the belfry stood an angel, bearing a golden crown, holding it out towards the said prince, to do him comfort. For the occasion, the conduits of the Cheap were painted in various colors and ran with red and white wine the whole time, so that anyone who wished could have to drink from them at any time. The said wine was transported by great pipes through which the wine moved without any being spilled. The said prince rode on through Fleetstreet, all the way to the palace at Westminster, there to repose himself and take rest, and the other lords went back into London, and thence about their hostelries.]

Appendix 3

Dymmok on the Ricardian Extravagance

In Gervase Mathew's view, "Richard's need for personal magnificence had probably always been combined with a ravaging extravagance."[1] The king's excesses were widely criticized at the time, in such learned and official sources as Walsingham's historical writings and parliamentary petitions, including the "Record and Process" of Richard's deposition, as well as such relatively popular vernacular writings as the poems "On the Times," *Richard the Redeless*, and *Mum and the Sothsegger*. The Ricardian extravagance had an apologist, too: the Dominican Roger Dymmok, whose father and brother acted as royal champions of England. In about 1395, Dymmok answered the widely-circulated vernacular "Lollard Twelve Conclusions" with his Latin tract *Contra XII errores et hereses lollardorum*.[2] The twelfth and final section of Dymmok's work contains arguments justifying the royal extravagance, a subject that the Lollard "Conclusions" had touched on obliquely. Perhaps most notable among Dymmok's arguments is the claim that kingly magnificence was a needful counter-revolutionary measure given present circumstances: "In fact," Dymmok writes, "it is obligatory for the kinds of lords whose job it is to rule peoples, in order that they might strike fear into their peoples, lest they rise up against their superiors too readily."[3] According to this line of thinking, the more excessive the extravagance the better.

Dymmok's literary procedure may seem initially disorienting, especially given the exigencies of representing his work in translation. Dymmok's tract is a *compilatio*, a more or less formal, scholastic response to an unscholastic and possibly even anti-scholastic piece of vernacular writing. The brief "Lollard Twelve Conclusions" — only about twenty-three

---

[1] Mathew, *Court of Richard II*, p. 151.

[2] The textual history of the "Lollard Twelve Conclusions" is discussed in Anne Hudson, *Selections from English Wycliffite Writings*, pp. 150–51. Dymmok's response to the Lollards is discussed by Fiona Somerset, "Answering the *Twelve Conclusions*," pp. 52–76, reprinted in Somerset, *Clerical Discourse*, pp. 103–34. The import of the section on extravagance was noted by Eberle, "The Politics of Courtly Style," pp. 168–78; see also Bowers, "*Pearl* in Its Royal Setting," p. 120, and Saul, *Richard II*, pp. 355–57. For biographical infomation, see Dymmok, *Liber*, pp. xi–xv, and Emden, *Biographical Register* 1.617.

[3] See below, p. 111 (compare lines 28–30 of the Latin text).

hundred words in length — was published at first by posting copies of it up in public places. No text survives in such a form, however. The earliest witness is Dymmok's representation of the conclusions in his *Contra XII errores et hereses lollardorum*. Dymmok begins each of the twelve chapters of his book by quoting one of the Lollard conclusions in full, in the original Middle English. Next, he translates the Middle English conclusion into his own Latin ("Which remarks are rendered in Latin as follows," in the section translated below), sometimes introducing changes that become significant in the ensuing discussions. Finally, still in Latin, Dymmok treats various arguments for and against the particular conclusion, in the *pro* and *contra* form made standard by Thomas Aquinas, for example, whose *Summa theologica* Dymmok uses extensively for making his anti-Lollard *compilatio*.

The text provided here is that of the first six chapters of the twelfth section of Dymmok's tract (printed by Cronin, pp. 292–304), though modernized both in basic orthography (*u/v* and *i/j*, for example) and in the punctuation of quoted material. It is possible to amend Cronin's Latin text, particularly by reference to the sources that Dymmok was using; such corrections are enclosed in angled brackets "<>" in the text following. The Modern English translation incorporates the corrections tacitly.

Against the Twelve Errors and Heresies of the Lollards

Part Twelve

[The Twelfth Conclusion distributed by the Lollards:]

Þe xii. conclusiun is þat, þe multitude of craftis nout nedful usid in our Chirche norsschith michil synne in wast, curosite and disgysing. Þis schewith experience and resun provith, for nature with a fewe craftis sufficith to nede of man. Þe correlari is, þat sytthin seynt Powel seyth, we havende oure bodili fode and hilling we schulde holde us apayed, us thinketh þat goldsmethis and armoreris and alle manere craftis nout nedeful to man aftir þe apostle schulde ben distroyd for þe encres of vertu. For þou þese to craftis nemlid were michil more nedful in þe elde lawe, þe newe testament hath voydid þese and manie othere.

[Dymmok's Latin translation of the Lollards' conclusion:]

Que in Latinum transfertur in hunc modum. Duodecima conclusio: Multitudo artium non necessariarum homini in nostra ecclesia multum peccatum nutrit in superflua curiositate et disfiguracione hominum per vestes curiosas. Hoc ostendit experiencia et racio probat, quia natura cum paucis artibus sufficeret humane nature. Correlarium:
5   Ex quo apostolus Paulus dicit, "Habentes victum et quibus tegamur, hiis contenti simus," nobis videtur quod aurifabri et fabri armorum et omnia genera artium non necessaria homini secundum apostolum destrui deberent propter augmentum virtutum.

Lines 1–9: Which remarks are rendered in Latin as follows. The Twelfth Conclusion: The multitude of arts not needful to man in our church nourishes much sin, by way of superfluous curiosity and people's disfigurement with curious vestment. So much experience shows and reason proves, for Nature herself, with few crafts, suffices for humankind. The corollary comes from what the apostle Paul says: "And having food and raiment, let us be therewith content." It seems to us that goldsmiths and armourers, and indeed all manner of arts not needful for humankind, by the Apostle's criteria, ought to be utterly wiped out, for the sake of virtues' augmentation. Howbeit that the

Quia quamvis iste due artes nominate necessarie fuerunt in veteri lege, novum tamen testamentum has artes cum multis aliis evacuavit.

[Dymmok's response to the Lollards:] Capitulum primum.

10   In ista xiiᵃ conclusione intendunt isti veritatis adversarii varias artes mechanicas adnullare pro eo, ut asserunt earum plurimas non necessarias ad victum et vestitum humane nature, et quia hominibus, ut dicunt, occasionem prebent peccandi in superfluo apparatu ad sui corporis decorem et superbie nutrimentum. Igitur ad intelligenciam eorum, que sequuntur, est notandum secundum Thomam (*Secunda Secunde*, q. cliᵃ,

15   articulo viii°, ad secundum⁴): Quod necessitas humane vite potest attendi duppliciter; uno modo, secundum quod est necessarium illud, sine quo res nullo modo esse potest, sicud cibus est necessarius animali. Et isto modo valde pauce artes sufficerent sive necessarie essent humane nature, quia natura humana paucis est contenta. Alio modo dicitur necessarium aliquid humane vite, secundum quod dicitur illud, sine quo res

20   non potest convenienter esse et isto modo, presupposita diversitate statuum et graduum

---

two arts here named were needful under the Old Law, the New Testament has yet voided these arts, as well as numerous others.

Chapter one.

Lines 10–23: By this their twelfth conclusion, these enemies of the truth mean to do away with the various crafts and arts, inasmuch as they assert that the most part of them are not needful for feeding and clothing humankind, and because — so they say — the crafts and arts, by their superfluous encumbrance, serve men up occasion for sinning, through means of the body's decoration and the fostering of pride thereby. Wherefore, for their better understanding, the following is to be taken into account. According to St. Thomas (2a2ae.151.8⁴), "necessity," in respect of human life, can be understood in two ways. In the first place, it can be understood in the sense that that without which a something can by no means exist is said to be "necessary," as food is necessary for the animate. In this perspective, a small number of the crafts would indeed suffice, or would be "necessary," for humankind can be content with little. In the second place, something can be said to be "necessary" for human life, in the sense that that may be said to be "necessary" without which a something cannot exist properly; and in this perspective, given the diversity of human estates and de-

---

⁴ The following distinction appears, in fact, to come from *Summa Theologica* 2a2ae.32.6.

et dignitatum hominum, valde multe artes sunt necessarie humane nature, secundum quod necesse est hominibus in victu et vestitu et in edificiis ordinari, secundum sui status decenciam et sue complexionis necessitatem. Oportet namque reges, principes et alios in sublimitatibus constitutos in edificiis magnifice decorari, prout probat

25 Philosophus (in iiii° *Etichorum*); scilicet necesse est eos habere edificia sumptuosa, magna, pulcra et bene ornata, ad quorum ornatum varii artifices requiruntur, scilicet pictores, sculptores, vitriarii, fabri, aurifices et alia genera artificum, que iam nimis longum esset enarrare. Et quod hoc competit talibus dominis, qui populum habent gubernare, ostendit Philosophus (vi° *Politicorum*), ad incuciendum metum populis, ne

30 nimis faciliter insurgant contra suos superiores. Cum enim talia subtilia et forcia populi et pulcra prospiciunt edificia principum, ipsos opulentos et industrios reputabunt, et tantum in potencia et sapiencia populum excellere, quod inpossibile reputabunt contra eos prevalere. Non solum autem in edificiis oportet eos multum excellere, set eciam in esculentis et poculentis. Cum enim universa genera ciborum facta sunt ad humane

35 nature sustentacionem, prout patet Gen. ii° et ix°, iustum est, ut persone digniores

---

grees and achievements, very many crafts are "necessary" for humankind, inasmuch as it is needful for men to be ranked in order, by means of their victualing and clothing and their housing, according to the decency of their respective estates and the necessity of their respective ways of life.

Lines 23–38: It is right, for example, that kings, princes, and others who have been set up in states of social elevation should have their estates dignified, indeed magnificently, by the kind of buildings they live in, as the Philosopher himself has asserted (in *Ethics* 4): namely, it is necessary for such men to inhabit buildings that are sumptuous, grand, comely, and thoroughly well decorated, for the proper decoration of which are required a variety of artisans, namely, painters, carvers, glaziers, smiths, jewelers, and artisans of other sorts, too, which it would indeed take too long to enumerate. Furthermore, the Philosopher (*Politics* 6) has likewise proven that such is in fact obligatory for the kinds of lords whose job it is to rule peoples, in order that they might strike fear into their peoples, lest they rise up against their superiors too readily. For when peoples can see that the residences of their princes are wrought with such skill and power and magnificence, they will regard their rulers as wealthy and competent, and they will regard overthrowing them as a thing so far impossible, to just that degree that their princes are seen to stand above their peoples in power and wisdom. Moreover, not only is it right that they should be seen to stand above their peoples in the way that they are housed, but likewise in the way that they eat and drink. Since in fact all varieties of foodstuffs were created for the sustenance of humankind, as is clear in Genesis 2 and 9, it is consequently just that persons of greater dignity should

ceteros precellant in sumptu ciborum et potuum et in ipsorum subtiliori apparatu, ad que paranda ars multiplex coquinaria requiritur, sine qua eciam, quantum ad necessitatem primo modo dictam, humana natura sufficeret sustentari. Et sic oportet principes ac nobiles secundum sui status decenciam in edificiis et esculentis excellencius ordinari

40   delicaciusque nutriri quam residuum populi; ita eciam oportet ipsos amplius quam ceteros diverso ornatu vestium decorari, non enim est congruum racioni, quod ita splendide vestiatur servus ut dominus, simplex miles ut princeps, monachus ut secularis, set sicud distinguntur homines in statibus et dignitatibus, sic racio exigit, ut diversorum vestimentorum apparatu distinguantur. Unde in *Secretis Secretorum* mandavit Aristoteles

45   Alexandro, quod nunquam populo publice appareret, nisi in decenti habitu ac splendenti, ut ex hoc in maiori apud eos reverencia haberetur. Quod autem habitus vilis facit personas in maiori quoad populum haberi contemptu, patet in vita beatorum apostolorum Symonis et Iude, ubi legitur, quod sapientes ad regis consilium vocati videntes eos, Symonem scilicet et Iudam, vilissima veste indutos ceperunt in contemptu habere

50   eorum personas. Quod autem non solum licet personis magne dignitatis populum precellere in sumptuosis edificiis, culcioribus cibis et potibus, set eciam vestium decoratu

---

be seen to stand above the rest, in respect of the richness of what they eat and drink and the skillful provisioning of it, for the preparation of which is required a manifold culinary art, in the absence of which humankind might not be sufficiently sustained, according to the argument I made above, about "necessity" of the first type.

Lines 38–60: Thus it is right that princes and nobles, in accord with the decency of their estate, be housed in greater magnificence and fed more sumptuously than the remainder of the population; just so, it is likewise right that such be also arrayed more lavishly than the rest, in raiment of varied ornament. For it is not accordant to reason that a servant be dressed as splendidly as a lord, or an ordinary knight as a prince, or a monk as a secular. Rather, just as persons are distinguished from one another in estate and dignity, so reason requires that they be distinguished from one another also by means of different styles of dress. Hence in the *Secreta secretorum*, Aristotle enjoined Alexander never to appear to his people in public except in appropriate, indeed in magnificent array, that by consequence thereof he would be held in greater esteem. Moreover, that humble dress causes personages to be held in the more contempt, in respect of the people, is clear from the life of the blessed apostles Simon and Jude, where we read that the esteemed counselors, called to their king, on catching sight of Simon and Jude, dressed as they were in the humblest of clothes, took to holding their persons in contempt. Additionally, that it is proper for persons of great dignity to stand above the people, not only in their sumptuous dwelling-places and in their more

satis ostenditur III° Reg. X°, ubi sic: "Videns autem regina Saba omnem sapienciam Salomonis et domum, quam edificaverat, et cibos mense eius et habitacula servorum et ordinem ministrancium, vestesque eorum et pincernas ac holocausta, que offerebat
55 in domo Domini, non habebat ultra spiritum. Dixitque regi: Verus est sermo, quem audivi in terra mea super sermonibus tuis et super sapiencia tua," etc. Ex quibus patet, quod ad regem pertinet habere sumptuosa edificia et pulcra, cibaria lauta et decorem vestimentorum, cum ex hiis sapiencia Salomonis vere extitit commendata, que nullo modo fieri potuerunt absque magna industria artificum, non necessario requisitorum
60 ad victum parcum hominum et eorum abiectum vestimentum.

Capitulum secundum.

Et quamvis licitum sit hominibus secundum sui status congruenciam tam in edificiis, quam in esculentis et vestibus, sumptuose ac subtiliter ordinari, tamen variis modis contingit homines in hiis omnibus virtutis medium transcendere, sicud docet sanctus

---

lavish food and drink, but also in the stateliness of their dress, is established well enough in 3 Kings 10:4–7, where we read:

> And when the queen of Sheba had seen all Solomon's wisdom, and the house that he had built, and the meat of his table, and the sitting of his servants, and the attendance of his ministers, and their apparel, and his cupbearers, and his ascent by which he went up unto the house of the Lord, there was no more spirit in her. And she said to the king, 'It was a true report that I heard in mine own land of thy acts and of thy wisdom.'

From these remarks, it is clear that for a king to have sumptuous, beautiful palaces, culinary splendor, and decorous dress is right and proper, since the very wisdom of Solomon here stands commended by reason of such things, as could in no wise be accomplished except by great industry on the part of artisans, certainly not by the necessity of the bare requisites of feeding people sparingly and clothing them poorly.

Chapter two.

Lines 61–75: Albeit it is lawful for some to be set apart from others, lavishly and artfully, by their dwelling-places, as well as by their clothing and dietary practices, in keeping with their estates, yet it does occasionally happen that, in all such matters, there may be persons who pass beyond the bounds of virtue, as St. Thomas teaches

Concordia facta inter regem et cives Londonie

Thomas (*Secunda Secunde*, q. CLXIX, articulo primo, in pede[5]) sic: "Quod in rebus
exterioribus, quibus homo utitur, non est vicium set ex parte hominis, qui immoderate
utitur eis, reperitur vicium." Que quidem immoderancia potest esse duplex; uno modo
quidem per comparacionem ad consuetudinem hominum, in quibus aliquis vivit. Unde
Augustinus dicit (in III° *Confessionum*): "Que contra mores hominum sunt flagicia pro
morum diversitate vitanda sunt." Alio modo potest immoderacio contingere in usu
talium rerum ex inordinato affectu utentis, ex quo quandoque contingit, quod homo
nimis libidinose talibus utitur, sive secundum consuetudinem eorum, cum quibus vivit,
sive eciam pr<e>ter eorum consuetudinem. Unde Augustinus dicit (in III° *De Doctrina
Christiana*): "In usu rerum abesse oportet libidinem, que non solum ipsa eorum, inter
quos vivit, consuetudine abutitur nequiter, set eciam sepe fines eius egressa feditatem
suam, que intra claustra morum omnium latebat, flagiciosissima erupcione manifestat."

65
70
75

(2a2ae.169[5]): "There is no moral evil in the things we make use of, but only in the
persons who use them immoderately." This immoderation can be seen to be twofold:
in the first place, in respect of the customs of the persons among whom someone
lives, whence Augustine says (*Confessions* 3): "While yet allowing for their diversity,
outrages against accepted manners are to be avoided." In the second place, immod-
eration results from inordinate affection in the use of such things on the part of the
person using them. By consequence, it sometimes occurs that a person makes use of
such things excessively libidinously, whether in keeping with the customs of the per-
sons amongst whom he lives or whether above and beyond those customs. Hence
Augustine says (*On Christian Doctrine* 3): "Disorderly passion in the use of things
needs be shunned, not only by abusing the customs of those amongst whom we live,
but also often by going too far and displaying in shameful discharge the filth which
before was hidden in the privy of received manners."

---

[5] Though the presentation in Cronin's edition (pp. 295–301) is not clear on this
point, the whole of the following chapters two through four — which is to say, over
half of Dymmok's twelfth section, on extravagance, chapters one through six — includ-
ing the scriptural and partristic quotations, is taken over wholesale from the section of
Aquinas mentioned here: *Summa theologica* 2a2ae.169, with a few omissions and a
verbal change or two (possibly verbal variations current in the textual tradition of St.
Thomas). See Somerset, "Answering the *Twelve Conclusions*," p. 75n28 (reprinted in
Clerical Discourse and Lay Audience, p. 121n29).

114

Contingit autem illa inordinacio affectus tripliciter, quantum ad superabundanciam, uno modo per hoc, quod homo ex superfluo cultu vestium hominum gloriam querit, prout scilicet vestes et alia huiusmodi ad exteriorem pertinent ornatum. Unde Gregorius dicit in quadam omelia: "Sunt nonnulli, qui cultum subtilium preciosarumque vestium

80   putant non esse peccatum, quod videlicet si culpa non esset, nequaquam sermo Dei tam vigilanter exprimeret, quod dives, qui torquebatur apud inferos, bisso et purpura indutus fuisset. Nemo quippe vestimenta precipua, scilicet excedencia proprium statum, nisi ad inanem gloriam querit." Alio modo, secundum quod homo per superfluum cultum vestium querit delicias, secundum quod vestes ordinantur ad corporis fomentum.

85   Tercio modo, secundum quod nimiam sollicitudinem apponit quis ad exteriorem vestium cultum, eciam si non sit aliqua deordinacio ex parte finis; et secundum hoc Andronicus ponit tres virtutes circa exteriorem cultum, scilicet humilitatem, que excludit intencionem glorie, unde dicit, quod humilitas est habitus non superabundans in sumptibus et preparacionibus; et per se sufficienciam, que excludit intencionem deliciarum, unde

90   dicit per se sufficiencia est habitus contentus, quibus oportet, et determinativa eorum,

---

Lines 76–86: Inasmuch as it is a matter of excess, this kind of inordinate affection results from three things, in the first place, when by overmuch attention to matters of dress, particularly clothing and other things of the sort, pertaining to personal adornment, a person courts the glory of the world. Hence Gregory says, in one of his homilies:

> There are those who believe that the cultivation of precious and costly clothing is no sin, but surely, if it were no sin, the word of God would by no means be so solicitous to make the point that Dives, subject to infernal torment, had dressed himself in purple and fine linen. No one uses ostentatious dress, namely, dress beyond what is appropriate for his estate, except for vainglory.

Secondly, inasmuch as their clothing is intended for bodily excitement, to that same extent persons use vestimentary fineries for pleasure. In the third place, inasmuch as what end can there be to excessive solicitude over vestimentary cultivation of the exterior, if not some sort of perturbation, at least to a degree?

Lines 86–95: On these accounts, Andronicus posits three principles for cultivation of the exterior, as follows. In the first place is humility, which precludes any intention of vainglory; and he says that this humility consists in a manner of self-presentation not superabundant in ornaments and preparations. Next comes sufficiency unto oneself, which precludes any intention of preciousness; and he says that sufficiency unto oneself consists in a manner of self-presentation that is content with what is proper, subject to determination by such things as pertain to sustaining life, in keeping with

que ad vivere contingit, secundum illud Apostoli (prima ad Thi. ult.): "Habentes alimenta et quibus tegamur, hiis contenti simus"; et simplicitatem, que excludit superfluam sollicitudinem, unde dicit, quod simplicitas habitus contentus est hiis, que contingunt.

95 Cum quibus omnibus stat quantumcunque solempnis apparatus vestium conveniens statui hominis debitis circumstanciis usitatus absque peccato. Alio modo ex parte defectus potest esse duplex deordinacio secundum affectum; uno modo ex necligencia hominis, qui non adhibet studium vel diligenciam ad hoc, quod exteriori cultu utatur, sicud oportet. Unde dicit Philosophus (vii° *Etichorum*); quod ad molliciem pertinet, quod aliquis trahat vestimentum per terram, ut non laboret elevando ipsum; alio modo,

100 secundum quod defectum ipsum vestium ordinat ad gloriam. Unde Augustinus (in libro *De Sermone Domini in Monte*) dicit: "Non solum in rerum corporearum nitore atque pompa, set eciam in ipsis sordibus luctuosis esse posse iactanciam, et eo periculosiorem, quo sub nomine servitutis Dei deci<p>it"; et Philosophus dicit (x° *Etichorum*), quod superabundancia <et> inordinatus defectus ad iactanciam pertinet.

105 Et sicud homines se possunt licite secundum sui status congruenciam ornare sumptuose et artificiose, ita artifices talium ornamentorum licite possunt suas artes exercere, et

---

that remark of the Apostle (1 Timothy 6:8): "And having food and raiment, let us be therewith content." The third is simplicity, which precludes superfluities of solicitude; he says that simplicity consists in a manner of self-presentation that contents itself with whatever comes. It is on all such considerations that rests the matter of considerate vestimentary array, of whatever sort, proper to a person's estate, appropriately fit to circumstance, and without sin.

Lines 95–104: From the other perspective, vestimentary defect can be regarded as a two-fold perturbation, in some measure, depending on what causes it. On the one hand, it comes of neglect, on the part of a person who is more careless or heedless than is proper, when it comes to the maintenance of appearances. Whence the Philosopher says (*Ethics* 7) that it amounts to laziness, should a person trail his cloak in the dirt and not trouble about lifting it up. On the other hand, vestimentary defect is a perturbation to the degree that the very defect aims at vainglory. Whence Augustine says (*On the Lord's Sermon on the Mount*), "In bodily things not only dazzle and pomp but also dirt and drabness can be ostentatious, and all the more insidiously as deceiving under guise of service to God." And the Philosopher says (*Ethics* 10) that both superabundance and inordinate neglect amount to arrogance.

Lines 105–8: So, just as persons can lawfully array themselves sumptuously and artfully, in keeping with the proprieties of their estates, by the same token the artisans who make such adornment possible can lawfully pursue their crafts; moreover, such

tales artifices non sunt destruendi set permittendi et fovendi, ut necessarii coadiutores hominum in conversacione eorum politica et civili.

Capitulum tercium.

110

115

120

Set contra predicta argui potest sic: Ex premissis enim sequi videtur, quod mulieres absque peccato mortali se ornare possent cultu mulierum usitato; set quod hoc sit falsum, arguitur sic: Primo, omne, quod est contra preceptum legis divine, est peccatum mortale; set ornatus mulierum usitatus, ut videtur, est contra preceptum legis divine, dicitur enim (prima Petri iiiº): "Quarum scilicet mulierum non sit extrinsecus, capillatura aut circumdacio auri aut indumenti vestimentorum cultus," ubi dicit glosa Cipriani: "Serico et purpura indute Christum non possunt induere, auro et margaritis ornate et monilibus ornamenta mentis et corporis perdiderunt." Set hoc non fit, nisi per peccatum mortale; igitur talis ornatus mulierum non potest esse sine peccato mortali.

Item, Ciprianus dicit (in libro *De Habitu Virginum*): "Non virgines tantum et viduas set et nuptas puto eciam esse omnes omnino feminas admonendas, quod opus Dei et facturam eius et plasma nullo modo adulterare debent, adhibito flavo colore vel nigro

---

artisans are to be not done away with, but allowed or even encouraged, as needful collaborators for persons who would carry out their social and civic duties.

Chapter three.

Lines 109–17: Against the aforesaid, however, it can be argued as follows, for from such premises it seems to be entailed that women can adorn themselves, with the kind of adornments customary for women, without any mortal sin. But that such would be false is proven thus. In the first place, everything that is contrary to the precept of holy writ is mortal sin. Women's customary adornment, however, is contrary to the precept of holy writ, apparently, for we read (1 Peter 3:3): "Whose adorning, let it not be that outward adorning of plaiting the hair, and of the wearing of gold, or of the putting on of robes," where the Gloss echoes Cyprian's remark: "women who have put on Christ cannot put on purple and fine linen; women who decorate themselves with gold and jewelry and pearls have put aside their proper adornments of mind and body." But such cannot be, except by mortal sin. Therefore, this kind of adornment of women cannot be without mortal sin.
Lines 118–26: Elsewhere, in his work *On the Comportment of Virgins*, Cyprian writes, "Not merely virgins and widows, but also wives and indeed all women should be admonished in no way to deface God's work and fabric, the clay that he fashioned,

pulvere vel rubeo, aut quolibet alio vera lineamenta corumpere medicamine"; et postea subdit: "Manus Deo inferunt, quando illud, quod ille formavit, reformare contendunt; impugnacio illa Dei operis est, prevaricacio et veritatis. Deum videre non poteris, cum oculi tibi non sint, quos fecit Deus set quos Diabolus infecit. De inimico tuo reperta

125 es, pariter arsura cum illo" — set hoc non debetur, nisi peccato mortali. Igitur ornatus mulierum non est sine peccato mortali.

Propterea, sicud non congruit mulieri, quod veste virili utatur, ita nec ei congruit, quod cultu inordinato utatur. Set primum est peccatum, dicitur enim (Deut. xxii°): "Non induatur mulier veste virili nec vir veste muliebri"; igitur videtur, quod eciam

130 superfluus ornatus mulierum sit peccatum mortale. Set contra hoc est, quod secundum hoc videretur, quod artifices huiusmodi ornamenta preparantes mortaliter peccarent. Responsio: Dicendum secundum Thomam (*Secunda secunde*, q. CLXIX^a, articulo II°, in pede): Quod circa ornamenta mulierum sunt ead<e>m attendenda, que sunt communiter dicta circa exteriorem cultum, et insuper quoddam aliud speciale, quia scilicet muliebris

135 cultus viros ad lasciviam provocat secundum illud Prov. VII°: "Ecce mulier occurrit

---

with the aid of golden cream, black shadow, and rouge, or by applying any cosmetic to alter the natural lineaments"; and he adds further on:

> They lay hands on God when they strive to reshape what He has shaped. This is an assault on His handiwork, a distortion of the truth. Thou shalt not be able to see God, having no longer the eyes that God made, but the eyes that the devil unmade; with him shalt thou burn on whose account thou art made up.

But such cannot be, except by mortal sin. Therefore, women's adornment is not without mortal sin.

Lines 127–30: Moreover, just as it fits not a woman to use men's clothing, no more does it fit her to use excessive ornament. The former is a sin, for it is written (Deuteronomy 22:5): "The woman shall not wear that which pertaineth unto a man, neither shall a man put on a woman's garment." It appears here too, therefore, that women's superfluous adornment is mortal sin.

Lines 130–31: Contrary to this, however, is that it would seem that artisans manufacturing adornments of this sort should on this account sin mortally.

Lines 132–40: The response, in keeping with the remarks of St. Thomas (2a2ae.169.2), is that, although all the same considerations, applying generally in respect to exterior adornment, need be taken into account, when it comes to women's ornament, there needs to be additionally further special consideration taken, precisely because feminine adornment provokes men to lust, in accord with the words of Proverbs (7:10):

ornatu meretricio preparata ad decipiendas animas." Potest tamen mulier licite operam dare ad hoc, ut viro suo placeat, ne per eius contemptum in adulterium labatur (prima ad Cor. vıı°): "Mulier, que nupta est, cogitat, que mundi sunt, quomodo placeat viro," et ideo, si coniugata ad hoc se ornet, ut viro suo placeat, potest hoc facere absque

140 peccato. Ille autem mulieres, que viros non habent nec volunt habere et sunt in statu non habendi, non possunt absque peccato appetere placere virorum aspectibus ad concupiscendum, quia hoc est eis dare incentivum peccandi. Et si quidem hac intencione se ornent, ut alios provocent ad concupiscenciam, peccant mortaliter. Si autem ex quadam animi levitate hoc faciant vel eciam propter vanitatem, scilicet propter quandam

145 animi iactanciam, non semper est peccatum mortale, set quandoque veniale, et eadem racio, quantum ad hoc, est de viris. Unde Augustinus dicit (in *Epistola ad Possidium*): "Nolo ut de ornamentis auri et vestis propriam habeas in prohibendo scienciam, ut in eos, qui neque coniugati sunt neque coniugari cupientes, cogitare debere, quomodo placeant Deo. Alii autem cogitant, quomodo placeant mundo, scilicet quomodo vel viri

150 uxoribus vel uxores viris, nisi quod capillos nudare feminas, quas eciam capud velare Apostolus iubet, nec eciam decet maritatas." In quo tamen possunt alique a peccato

---

"And behold there met him a woman with the attire of a harlot, and subtile of heart." A woman can yet lawfully put effort into such, in order to please her husband, lest he be fallen into adultery for contempt of her: "But she that is married careth for the things of the world, how she may please her husband" (1 Corinthians 7:34). Therefore, should a wife adorn herself to please her husband for such a purpose, she can do so without sin.

Lines 140–46: On the other hand, such women as have no husbands, or want no husbands and are of such estate as not to have husbands, cannot without sin set about to please men's gazes to the point of inciting lust, for such is to give men incentive to sin. If any should adorn themselves with such an intention, in order to incite others' lust, they would sin mortally. If, on the other hand, for simple-minded light-heartedness or even plain vanity, namely, out of willful pride, should any do so, it is not always a mortal sin, but may be sometimes only venial; and the same rationale applies to men, too.

Lines 146–53: Hence Augustine writes, in the *Letter to Possidius*,

> I should not wish you to make any impulsive regulation forbidding the use of jewelry or fine clothing, except that those who are neither married nor desirous of being married ought to be thinking about how to please God. But worldly people think of worldly things: if husbands, how to please their wives; if wives, how to please their husbands. However, it is not seemly for women, even married ones, to uncover their hair, since the Apostle commands them to veil their heads.

excusari, quando non fit ex aliqua vanitate set propter contrariam consuetudinem, quamvis talis consuetudo non sit laudabilis. Ex quibus sequitur, quod mulieres nupte et nubere disponentes possunt licite uti quibuscunque ornamentis usitatis a feminis sui status et apud eas consuetis, dummodo hoc non faciant perversa intencione ad alliciendum homines ad concupiscenciam illicitam, nec propter pompam aut iactanciam, set tantum, ut placeant viris suis habitis vel habendis, seu ut aliorum, cum quibus conversantur, moribus se conforment. Et idem per omnia de viris est dicendum.

155

Capitulum quartum.

Ad primum igitur dicendum est, quod, sicud Glosa ibidem dicit, mulieres eorum, qui in tribulacione erant, contempnebant viros suos et, ut aliis placerent, se pulcrius ornabant, et hoc prohibuit apostolus Petrus ibidem. In quo eciam casu loquitur Ciprianus, et hoc usque in hodiernum diem a mulieribus observatur. Quando enim viri sui sunt in partibus remotis aut in quacunque angustia constituti, non ornant se margaritis aut aliis pulcris suis ornamentis. Non autem prohibet Apostolus coniugatis, ut placeant

160

On this point, however, a woman may be excused from sin when without vanity she follows the prevailing contrary custom, although such a custom is not to be commended.

Lines 153–58: From all of which it follows, that married women, as well as women intending to marry, can lawfully use whatever adornment is used by women of their estate and is customary among them, provided that they do so, not with a perverted intention of seducing men to illicit lust, nor for pomp and glory, but only in order to please their husbands or husbands to be, or in order to conform themselves to what is customary amongst the persons with whom they must interact; and all the same points apply to men.

Chapter four.

Lines 159–74: In the first place, it must therefore be pointed out, as the Gloss says at the same point, that the wives of men who were in distress despised their husbands and, in order to attract other men, adorned themselves more pleasingly than usual; this the apostle Peter forbids. Of such a circumstance, Cyprian spoke, and the same practice is used by women even up to the present day. For when their husbands are away in distant parts, or are subject to difficulties of any sort, they ought not adorn themselves with pearls or other ornamental fineries of theirs. Lest occasion for sinning with other women be given them, the Apostle does not forbid spouses from

165   viris, ne detur eis occasio peccandi cum aliis. Unde Apostolus (prima ad Timo. ii°)
docuit "mulieres in habitu ornato orare cum verecundia et sobrietate, non in tortis
crinibus aut auro aut margaritis aut veste preciosa." Per quod datur intelligi, quod
sobrius et moderatus vestium cultus non prohibetur mulieribus set superfluus et
inverecundus et impudicus, qualis est omnis ornatus statum mulieris excedens, et
170   adhibitus ei propter concupiscenciam augmentandam inordinate vel ad illam inordinate
excitandam, et solum talis. Unde Glosa super eodem textu Apostoli ibidem: "Non
sint," inquid, "mulieres ornantes se veste preciosa," etc., ut in hiis omnibus ultra
persone sue modulum et mores occasione movende concupiscencie studeant, set
pocius sint promittentes pietatem per opera bona.

175   Ad secundum dicendum, quod mulierum futacio, de qua Ciprianus loquitur, est
quedam species fictionis, que non potest esse sine peccato. Unde Augustinus dicit (in
Epistola ad Possidium): "Fucari pigmentis, quo rubicundior vel candidior appareat,
adulterina fallacia est, qua non dubito eciam ipsos maritos se decipi nolle, quibus solis
permittende sunt femine ornari solis, scilicet viris habitis vel habendis, secundum
180   veniam, non secundum imperium." Non tamen semper talis futacio est cum peccato

---

pleasing their husbands. On this point, the Apostle teaches (1 Timothy 2:9): "I would
that women pray adorned in modest apparel, with shamefacedness and sobriety, not
with braided hair, or gold, or pearls, or costly array." By this remark is given to
understand that, though grave and moderate vestmental ornament is not forbidden
women, the excessive or the immodest or the shameless is, including all adornment
that goes beyond what is appropriate to the woman's estate, and all adornment that
she puts on to augment lust inordinately, or inordinately to incite to lust: thus much
only is prohibited. So says the Gloss on this same apostolic text: "women ought not,"
it says, "to be found dressing themselves in finery," and so forth, and in all the like,
above the mode and manner proper to their persons, with the intention of stirring lust,
but rather they ought to put themselves forward in piety by means of good works.
Lines 175–86: In the second place, it must be pointed out that women's face-paint-
ing, of which Cyprian speaks, is a species of fiction, the kind of thing that cannot be
without sin. Whence Augustine says, in the *Letter to Possidius*,

> As to the practice of painting their faces to make them more pink and white, I doubt
> that even their own husbands care to be deceived, and husbands — actual or
> prospective — are the only men for whom women are allowed to deck themselves
> out, and that by indulgence, not command.

mortali, set solum quando fit propter lasciviam, vel in Dei contemptum, in quibus casibus loquitur Ciprianus. Sciendum est tamen, quod aliud est fingere pulcritudinem non habitam, et aliud est occultare turpitudinem ex aliqua causa provenientem, puta, egritudine vel aliquo huiusmodi. Hoc est enim licitum secundum Apostolum (prima ad
185 Cor. xº): "Que putamus ignobiliora esse membra corporis, hiis honorem abundanciorem circumdamus."

Ad tercium dicendum, sicud dictum est: Cultus exterior debet convenire condicioni persone secundum communem consuetudinem, et ideo de se viciosum est, quod mulier utatur veste virili aut econtra, et precipue quia hoc potest esse causa lascivie et specialiter
190 prohibetur in lege antiqua, quia gentiles tales mutaciones habitus utebantur ad ydolatrie supersticionem. Potest tamen quandoque hoc fieri sine peccato, aliquando propter aliquam necessitatem, vel causa occultandi ab hostibus, vel propter defectum alterius vestimenti, vel propter aliquid huiusmodi.

Ad quartum dicendum, quod, si qua ars est ad facienda opera aliqua, quibus hom-
195 ines uti non possunt absque peccato, per consequens artifices talia faciendo peccarent, utpote prebentes aliis directe occasiones peccandi; puta, si quis fabricaret ydola vel aliqua ad cultum ydolatrie pertinencia, et secundum istum modum sunt omnes artes

---

Nonetheless, such face-painting does not always entail mortal sin, but does so only when it is undertaken for purposes of lust or in contempt of God, in the instances of which Cyprian speaks. Yet it needs be understood that it is one thing to feign a beauty one does not have, and it is something else again to cover over a defect, born of any cause, illness, for example, or something else of the sort. For such is lawful, according to the Apostle (1 Corinthians 12:23): "And those members of the body, which we think to be less honorable, upon these we bestow more abundant honour."

Lines 187–93: In the third place, it must be pointed out that, as has been said, exterior adornment must be appropriate to the person's condition, in keeping with established custom. Consequently, it is a vice, in and of itself, for a woman to dress like a man, and vice versa, especially inasmuch as such can be occasion for lust and is expressly prohibited in the Old Law, because the gentiles used such exchange of manners of dress by reason of idolatrous superstition. Nonetheless, such can at times be used without sin, whenever it is used by reason of necessity, by way of disguise from enemies, for example, or for a want of other clothing, and the like.

Lines 194–203: In the fourth place, it must be pointed out that, if there is any art used for making anything that men cannot put to use except in sin, the artisans do sin by consequence of the very act of making such, inasmuch as directly they provide others opportunity to sin, for example, were someone to fabricate idols or anything pertaining to an idolatrous cult; and in keeping with such reasoning all the forbidden

prohibite destruende, puta, geomancia, aeremancia, ydromancia, piromancia, nigromancia, ars divinativa, ars notaria, omnia sortilegia, alligature, observancie, vacca

200   Platonis, sigillum Salomonis et cetere figure in talibus artibus supersticiose facte, que omnia condempnantur in canone (cap. xxvi, per totum). Operibus namque istorum uti non possunt homines absque peccato, et ideo omnes tales artes illicite sunt et penitus destruende. Si qua vero ars sit, cuius operibus homines possunt bene et male uti, sicud gladii, sagitte et huiusmodi, usus talium artium non est peccatum, et hee artes

205   licite sole sunt dicende. Unde Crisostomus (*Super Math.*): "Eas solas oportet artes vocare, que necessariorum et eorum, que continent vitam nostram, sunt tributive et constructive." Si tamen operibus alicuius artis, ut pluries aliqui male uterentur, quamvis de se non sint illicite, sunt tamen per officium principis a civitate extirpande secundum documenta Platonis. Quia igitur mulieres possunt licite ornare se, vel ut conservent

210   decenciam sui status, vel aliquid eciam superaddere, ut placeant viris, consequens est, quod artifices talium ornamentorum non peccant in usu talis artis, nisi forte inveniendo aliqua superflua et curiosa; unde Crisostomus dicit (*Super Matheum*), quod "ab arte calceariorum et textorum multa absc<i>ndere oportet, etenim ad luxuriam deduxerunt, necessitatem eius corumpentes arte mala arti commiscentes."

---

arts are fit for destruction, such as, for example, divinations by earth, by air, by water, and by fire; necromancy; divining and the magical art notary; all forms of sorcery, amulet-tying, and spell-casting; the Platonic wand, the seal of Solomon, and the rest of the tokens used superstitiously in arts of this sort. All of them are condemned by the canon law (cap. 26); for men cannot put arts of this sort to use except in sin, and therefore all such arts are unlawful and fit for utter destruction.

Lines 203–14: On the other hand, if there be any art used for making things that men can put to use either for good or for ill — such as swords or arrows or the like — the employment of such arts is no sin, and such arts alone can be said to be lawful. Whence Chrysostom (*On Matthew*) says: "Only those that produce and contribute to the necessities and mainstays of life should be called arts." By way of contrast, if, as often enough happens, some make use of the products of an art for ill purposes, even if the products themselves be not unlawful per se, yet it falls to the duty of the prince to see to it that they be driven out of the city, according to the doctrine of Plato. Therefore, since women can lawfully adorn themselves, in order to safeguard the decencies of their estates, or can lawfully even add something to their beauty, in order to please their husbands, the conclusion is that the artisans who work the means of such adornment do no sin in the cultivation of their arts, unless perchance they work at anything superfluous or fantastic. Whence Chrysostom says, "Even the arts of the cobbler and the weaver need to be curtailed, for they have been drawn into lechery; the need for them has been corrupted, and art has been debased by artifice."

Capitulum quintum.

215   Ex quibus sequitur, quod lex evangelica nullas artes prohibuit, que licuerunt in veteri lege, nisi forte illas artes, que observate sunt in ceremoniis Iudeorum et ritu sacrificiorum veteris legis. Omnes enim artes, quarum opera fieri potuerunt ab hominibus absque peccato, licuerunt tunc, sicud et nunc. Alie vero artes, quarum opera fieri non possent absque peccato, tunc dampnate fuerunt, sicud patet de artibus prius recitatis (Deut.

220   XVIII° et primo Regum XXVIII° et IIII° Regum XXIII°). Nunc eciam eedem artes dampnantur, sicud patet ex preallegatis. Artes vero, quibus homines sepius male usi sunt, quam bene, fuerunt tunc, sicud et nunc, per principes a civitatibus expellende, quamvis de se licite fuissent, propter nocumentum reipublice.

    Aurifabri vero et fabri armorum, quas artes dicunt penitus destruendas, et in novo

225   testamento approbantur equaliter sicud in veteri testamento. De aurifabris patet, quando Christus non prohibuit nummismata, set ea approbavit mandando ea dari Cesari tanquam sua, que per aurifabros fiunt (Mathei XXII°); et ipsemet pecuniam habuit pro necessariis emendis (Ioh. XII°); et similiter Philosophus (primo et III° *Politicorum*) ostendit, quod

---

Chapter five.

Lines 215–23: From all such it follows that the law evangelical prohibits no art which was lawful under the old dispensation, unless perchance it be such arts as were used in the cults of the Jews and the rites of sacrifice of the old dispensation. All such arts, the products of which were capable of being put to use by men without sin, were lawful at that time, just as they are even now. On the other hand, such other arts, the products of which could not be put to use without sin, were condemned at that time, as is clear of the arts listed above (see also Deuteronomy 18, 1 Kings 28, and 4 Kings 23). Now too the same arts stand condemned, as is clear from the aforegoing. Additionally, as for those arts that men make use of for ill more often than for good, it fell then to princes, just as it does even now, to see to it that such be driven away, no matter that the arts themselves be not unlawful per se, because of the damage they do the commonwealth.

Lines 224–46: "Goldsmiths and armourers, however" — arts they say ought utterly to be done away with — are indeed "approved in the New Testament, just as they are in the Old." Such is clear in the case of goldsmiths, since Christ did not prohibit the use of coinage but gave it his approval, bidding "render unto Caesar the things which are Caesar's" (Matthew 22:21), specifically, goldsmiths' products. Moreover, Christ himself kept money, for seeing to necessities (see John 13:29). Likewise, the Philosopher shows (*Politics* 1 and 3) that it is necessary that there be money, for making

necesse est pecuniam esse propter commutaciones faciendas inter homines rerum
230 humane vite necessariorum, que absque aurifabri arte et diligencia non fiunt. Quod
autem ars aurifabrorum non sit abicienda, patet per hoc, quod Dominus per se et
immediate docuit artem illam et multas alias non solum ad necessitatem humane vite
requisitas, set eciam ad decorem divini cultus et hominum in dignitate constitutorum
(Exo. xxxi°): "Ecce vocavi ex nomine Bezeleel et implevi eum Spiritu Dei, sapiencia et
235 intelligencia et sciencia in omni opere fabre ad cogitandum quicquid fieri poterit ex
auro, argento et ere et marmore et gemmis et diversitate lignorum"; et in eodem libro
(a xxv° usque ad xxxi capitulum eiusdem libri) approbat et precipit fieri varia ornamenta
in pannis lineis, auro et argento, tam opere textario, polimitario et plumario, quam in
picturis et sculpturis ad decorem tabernaculi et ornatum ministrorum eius, quibus
240 artibus homines utuntur usque in hodiernum diem in ornamentis pannorum suorum et
femine in ornamentis capitis sui in serico, auro et argento et gemmis satis licite et
absque peccato. Igitur tales in novo testamento aut per evangelium prohibite non sunt,
et eo maxime quo Deus ipsas fieri mandavit; nec est aliqua racio sufficiens, quare
modo debeant huiusmodi artes prohiberi pocius quam in lege veteri. Igitur nunc, sicud

---

exchanges among men, of such things as are needful for human life: such could not
take place absent the goldsmith's art and application. Furthermore, that the gold-
smiths' art is not worthy to be cast out is clear also from the fact that the Lord himself
taught, directly, that their art and numerous others were requisite, not only for provid-
ing the necessities of human life, but additionally for adornment of the divine worship
and of such men as are set in estates of dignity (Exodus 31:2–5):

> See, I have called by name Bezaleel, and I have filled him with the spirit of God, in
> wisdom, and in understanding, and in knowledge, and in all manner of workman-
> ship, to devise cunning works, to work in gold, and in silver, and in brass, and in
> cutting of stones, and in carving of timber.

In the same biblical book, chapters twenty-five through thirty-one, he sanctions and
ordains the fabrication of various ornaments, of linen drapery, of gold and of silver,
the work of weavers, embroiderers, and featherers, as well as work at painting and
carving, for the decoration of the temple and the adornment of the ministers thereof.
Even unto the present day, men make use of these same arts for adorning their cloth-
ing, as do women, for adorning their whole persons, in silk, in gold and silver, and in
gems, lawfully enough and without sin. Such arts are therefore prohibited neither in
the New Testament nor by the Gospel, and for this reason above all, namely, that God
himself gave them mandate; nor is there any adequate reason why arts of this sort
ought now to be forbidden, any more than they were under the Old Law. Conse-

245   et tunc, tales artes sunt permittende et approbande. Legitur eciam sanctum
Dunstanum aurifabrum fuisse et multa vasa de auro et argento subtiliter fecisse.

Capitulum sextum.

Quod vero fabri armorum sunt necessarii et in novo testamento approbati, patet
per hoc, quod milicia licita est et necessaria inter Christianos, sicud patet ex hiis,
que dicta sunt in xᵃ parte, et per consequens oportet eos, scilicet milites, habere
250   omnia genera armorum tam defensivorum, quam invasivorum, cuius rei raciones
varias tunc adduxi, que arma fieri oportet industria fabrorum armorum, et per
consequens ars illa nedum est tolleranda inter Christianos, set eciam bona diligencia
nutrienda et servanda. Vegecius enim (*De Re Militari*) et Philosophus (viii°
Politicorum) ostendunt prudenciam militarem necessariam esse ad regni et populi
255   gubernacionem, ad quam pertinet eciam considerare et cognoscere omnia arma
bellica et instrumenta eius, artificesque armorum in suis operibus dirigere per
modum architectorum vel principantis in arte illa, et per consequens ars illa fac-

---

quently, now just as then, such arts are to be permitted and approved. It is even
written that St. Dunstan had been a goldsmith and had made many a vessel, skill-
fully, of gold and of silver.

Chapter six.

Lines 247–60: That arms-makers are needful and approved in the New Testa-
ment is apparent from the fact that soldiery is lawful and necessary amongst
Christians, as is apparent from the remarks made above in Part Ten, and conse-
quently it is right for them, namely soldiers, to have weapons of all types, both
defensive and offensive. The several justifications for such a state of affairs I
have adduced already: it is right for such arms to be produced though the industry
of arms-makers, and consequently their art, far from being only tolerable amongst
Christians, is rather indeed to be fostered and guarded with all due diligence.
Vegetius, in *The Military Affairs*, and the Philosopher too, in *The Politics* 8, dem-
onstrate that military acumen is indeed needful for governing realms and peoples.
To such governance pertains familiarity with and knowledge of all arms of war
and its sundry instruments, as well as supervision of arms-makers about their
tasks, after the fashion of architects, or of a master in their art. By consequence,

260 ture armorum non solum licita est set eciam necessaria, et per consequens nullo
modo destruenda. Nimia igitur temeritas est asserere illa destrui oportere, que
Deus providit hominibus ad usus necessarios profutura, cuiusmodi sunt prius
recitata, sicud patet per beatum Augustinum (libro xxii° *De Civitate*, capitulo xxiiii°),
ubi ostendit, quod homini animam dedit racionalem, qua mediante capax esset
omnium virtutum cardinalium et magnam habet industriam artes varias et
265 subtilissimas adinvenire humane vite necessarias, sicud in edificiis et vestimentis,
agricultura et fabricandis vasis, in capcione et edomacione piscium, volatilium et
ferarum, in pigmentariis, in musicis, in escis et potibus et salciamentis, picturis et
sculpturis et aliis multis ibidem recitatis, que, Deo cooperante, sunt invente et
hucusque ad hominum solacium usitate. Igitur qui ista impungnant, divinam
270 providenciam tollere conantur, qua nature humane de artibus illis providit in
supplecionem humane nature defectus, et promocionem politice conversacionis
inter homines, et ostensionem divine sapiencie in rebus disponendis, non solum in
naturali operacione set eciam disponendis, non solum in naturali operacione set
eciam in artificiali adinvencione et divine bonitatis multiplici communicacione.

---

the art of arms manufacture is not only lawful but is moreover needful; by conse-
quence, it is by no means to be done away with.

Lines 260–77: It is rashness of the most extreme sort, in fact, to assert that such
things as God has provided men, for their needful employments to come, ought by
rights to be done away with. Considerations of this sort have already been re-
hearsed, as St. Augustine makes clear, in *The City of God* 22.24, where he dem-
onstrates that God endowed man with a rational soul, by means of which man
should be able to grasp all the cardinal virtues and have great skill in discovering
sundry, subtle arts, needful for human life, as in clothing and housing himself,
agriculture and pottery-making, in catching and consuming fishes, fowls, and
wild beasts, in dye-making, in music, in cookery, brewery, and spicery, painting
and sculpture, and all the many other things there rehearsed — all of them, by
God's provision, being helps to man's welfare and are put to use for just such a
reason. Therefore, whoever attacks such things tries to abolish divine providence
— the divine providence that provided humankind with such arts as might make
good the defects of humankind, advance civil intercourse among men, and dem-
onstrate God's wisdom in setting things aright, not only by means of men's natu-
ral operations, but likewise by means of men's artful discoveries and their bounti-
ful manifestation of God's goodness therethrough. Deputing all the goods of na-

275 Cuius immense bonitati non suffecit solum ad nostrum usum omnia naturalia conferre, nisi eciam operacione arcium diversarum eas humanis profectibus applicari accomodacius ordinaret.[6]

---

ture to our disposal alone were not enough for the great bounty of God's goodness, had he not ordained too that such also be put more amply to use, for humankind's benefit, by application of the sundry arts.[6]

---

[6] The remaining chapters of Part Twelve, chapters 7–12, consist of summary of the twelve Lollard conclusions and Dymmok's hortatory general conclusions. His summary of the twelfth conclusion is: "In XII^a autem et ultima politicam hominum communicacionem, statuum ac graduum varietatem impediunt, dum docent pene omnes artes mechanicas removendas, omnes homines modo consimili vestiendos, parique pastu pascendos, et sic in quadam conclusione homines ponentes universos distinctionem ecclesie ordinem decoremque confundunt" ("In the twelfth and final conclusion, they impugn men's civil intercourse and distinctions of rank and estate, in teaching that almost all the mechanical arts are to be done away with, and that all men should be clothed in the same manner and fed alike; thus, making men all the same, they would end by overturning the church's distinction, order, and decency" — Dymmok, *Liber*, p. 305).]

Appendix 4

Some Features of Prosody and Versification

4.1 Lengthening before the strong caesura

9 Ricardē	175 crucibūs	304 vobīs	419 vestrā
30 inultūs	177 respirarē	308 placitē	427 aīt
61 coccineā	184 Australē	319 ibī	432 formā
62 celūm	194 eximiām	324 extaticūs	442 edictā
75 ornatūs	202 partē	328 sibī	450 efficerē
76 togā	216 suscipimūs	331 ibī	455 ornatūs
81 argentariūs	225 elegīt	333 dulcōr	456 difficilē
85 sartōr	230 vestēr	336 multimodūm	458 insolitā
89 vaginatōr	237 tegitūr	338 psalteriā	472 modō
91 pandoxatōr	239 dominā	342 michī	474 mortīs
104 propinquantē	240 instantēr	346 clerūs	478 prostratā
128 frontē	244 faciēs	355 incensūm	480 Arthurūs
139 vobīs	254 luxūs	358 portē	484 iniuriā
147 causā	267 ibī	361 spinetā	494 modō
151 ornatūs	273 foliā	392 suā	508 amōr
161 sequitūr	284 turrīs	397 patrissantē	535 maiōr
172 concussīt	286 scalā	408 veniā	

4.2 Shortening of final -*o*

12 gliscŏ	152 tendŏ	305 referendŏ	478 supplicŏ
16 supputŏ	174 venerandŏ	310 subridendŏ	487 rogŏ
16 dandŏ	241 referendŏ	350 concitŏ	493 sumŏ
49 processiŏ	253 rogŏ	365 leŏ	507 proteccĭŏ
50 ordŏ	281 putŏ	405 compassiŏ	516 sperŏ
86 mangŏ	288 nesciŏ	421 extendendŏ	518 ponderŏ
94 caupŏ	295 virgŏ	425 cernŏ	527 contenciŏ
96 putŏ	296 eloquendŏ	426 remittŏ	534 variandŏ

4.3 Shortening of final -*e*

157 valdĕ	304 intimĕ	354 dulcĕ	486 intimĕ
158 valdĕ	324 intimĕ	392 publicĕ	518 valdĕ

4.4 Short *e* from classical Latin *ae*

74 prĕest	141 vestrĕ	325 ĕtas

4.5 Initial *h-* closing a preceding syllable

28 nēc habet	168 priūs hec	234 tamēn hillari	303 quōd habet

4.6 Other unclassical quantities

7 sāta	168 posteriūs	314 quiĕtasse	457 Nām
16 numerūm	193 mirificūm	319 trōnus (com-	459 trōnus (com-
26 ŏdisse (com-	194 lŭcem	pare 459, 495)	pare 319, 495)
pare 146, 416)	201 dŭcit	331 melŏdia	460 tegmĭna
30 īnultus (but	201 dĕputatus	344 vĭsitare	476 humilīs
compare 414	209 nīmis (but	348 Ād	480 Quamvĭs
ĭnultus)	compare 111,	383 crucīfixi	489 plĕbibus
37 adōlescens	137, 198, 206,	416 ŏderit (com-	(compare 426,
105 credĭs	380 nĭmis)	pare 26, 146)	532)
126 bĕrillus	217 Concĕdimus	426 plĕbis (com-	495 mĕcum
130 trahīt	223 imperătoria	pare 489, 532)	495 trōnum (com-
138 prŏvoluti	232 salŭs	431 propăgata	pare 319, 459)
146 ŏderit (com-	245 gaudentēr	434 sōnat	514 auctŏritas
pare 26, 416)	263 Āt	443 quĭn	532 plĕbem (com-
165 Vīridibus	280 corŏnata	444 sītis	pare 426, 489)
166 bīpartitis	294 subtĭlitate	446 Auxiliūm	

Appendix 4

4.7 Patterns of dactyl (D) and spondee (S) distribution

In hexameters (first four feet), by (number of lines [of the total 274 hexameters]) and by percent, from most to least frequent:

1. DDDD (36): 13.1%
2. DDSD (34): 12.4%
2. DSDD (34): 12.4%
4. DSSD (30): 10.9%
5. DSDS (28): 10.2%
6. DSSS (25): 9.1%
7. DDDS (20): 7.3%
7. DDSS (20): 7.3%

9. SDSD (11): 4.0%
10. SDSS (8): 2.9%
10. SSSS (8): 2.9%
12. SDDD (6): 2.2%
12. SSDD (6): 2.2%
14. SDDS (3): 1.1%
14. SSDS (3): 1.1%
16. SSSD (2): 0.7%

In pentameters (first two feet), by (number of lines [of the total 272 pentameters]) and by percent, from most to least frequent:

1. DD (122): 44.9%
2. DS (104): 38.2%

3. SD (32): 11.8%
4. SS (14): 5.1%

Some comparable figures for Ovid's elegiac verse are in Maurice Platnauer, *Latin Elegiac Verse*, pp. 36–37; and for the long hexameter poems, from the earliest records to late antiquity, in George E. Duckworth, *Vergil and Classical Hexameter Poetry*, especially Table 1. For Anglo-Saxon-period Anglo-Latin poets, see Andy Orchard, "After Aldhelm," 96–133; and figures for some later medieval continental Latin poets are discussed in Warner of Rouen, *Moriuht*, ed. Christopher J. McDonough, especially pp. 60–61.

Volumes in the Middle English Texts Series

The Floure and the Leafe, The Assembly of Ladies, and *The Isle of Ladies,* ed. Derek Pearsall (1990)

Three Middle English Charlemagne Romances, ed. Alan Lupack (1990)

Six Ecclesiastical Satires, ed. James M. Dean (1991)

Heroic Women from the Old Testament in Middle English Verse, ed. Russell A. Peck (1991)

The Canterbury Tales: Fifteenth-Century Continuations and Additions, ed. John M. Bowers (1992)

Gavin Douglas, *The Palis of Honoure,* ed. David Parkinson (1992)

Wynnere and Wastoure and The Parlement of the Thre Ages, ed. Warren Ginsberg (1992)

The Shewings of Julian of Norwich, ed. Georgia Ronan Crampton (1993)

King Arthur's Death: The Middle English Stanzaic Morte Arthur and Alliterative Morte Arthure, ed. Larry D. Benson and Edward E. Foster (1994)

Lancelot of the Laik and Sir Tristrem, ed. Alan Lupack (1994)

Sir Gawain: Eleven Romances and Tales, ed. Thomas Hahn (1995)

The Middle English Breton Lays, ed. Anne Laskaya and Eve Salisbury (1995)

Sir Perceval of Galles and Ywain and Gawain, ed. Mary Flowers Braswell (1995)

Four Middle English Romances: Sir Isumbras, Octavian, Sir Eglamour of Artois, Sir Tryamour, ed. Harriet Hudson (1996)

The Poems of Laurence Minot (1333–1352), ed. Richard H. Osberg (1996)

Medieval English Political Writings, ed. James M. Dean (1996)

The Book of Margery Kempe, ed. Lynn Staley (1996)

Amis and Amiloun, Robert of Cisyle, and Sir Amadace, ed. Edward E. Foster (1997)

The Cloud of Unknowing, ed. Patrick J. Gallacher (1997)

Robin Hood and Other Outlaw Tales, ed. Stephen Knight and Thomas Ohlgren (1997)

The Poems of Robert Henryson, ed. Robert L. Kindrick (1997)

Moral Love Songs and Laments, ed. Susanna Greer Fein (1998)

John Lydgate, *Troy Book: Selections,* ed. Robert R. Edwards (1998)

Thomas Usk, *The Testament of Love,* ed. R. Allen Shoaf (1998)

Prose Merlin, ed. John Conlee (1998)

Middle English Marian Lyrics, ed. Karen Saupe (1998)

John Metham, *Amoryus and Cleopes,* ed. Stephen F. Page (1999)

Four Romances of England: King Horn, Havelok the Dane, Bevis of Hampton, Athelston, ed. Ronald B. Herzman, Graham Drake, and Eve Salisbury (1999)

The Assembly of Gods: Le Assemble de Dyeus, or Banquet of Gods and Goddesses, with the Discourse of Reason and Sensuality, ed. Jane Chance (1999)

Thomas Hoccleve, *The Regiment of Princes*, ed. Charles R. Blyth (1999)

John Capgrave, *The Life of St. Katherine*, ed. Karen Winstead (1999)

John Gower, *Confessio Amantis*, Vol. 1, ed. Russell A. Peck (2000); Vol. 2 (2003)

Richard the Redeless and *Mum and the Sothsegger*, ed. James Dean (2000)

Ancrene Wisse, ed. Robert Hasenfratz (2000)

Walter Hilton, *The Scale of Perfection*, ed. Thomas Bestul (2000)

John Lydgate, *The Siege of Thebes*, ed. Robert Edwards (2001)

Pearl, ed. Sarah Stanbury (2001)

The Trials and Joys of Marriage, ed. Eve Salisbury (2002)

Middle English Legends of Women Saints, ed. Sherry L. Reames (2003)

The Wallace: Selections, ed. Anne McKim (2003)

Other TEAMS Publications

Documents of Practice Series:

Love and Marriage in Late Medieval London, selected, translated, and introduced by Shannon McSheffrey (1995)

Sources for the History of Medicine in Late Medieval England, selected, introduced, and translated by Carole Rawcliffe (1995)

A Slice of Life: Selected Documents of Medieval English Peasant Experience, edited, translated, and with an introduction by Edwin Brezette DeWindt (1996)

Regular Life: Monastic, Canonical, and Mendicant Rules, selected with an introduction by Douglas J. McMillan and Kathryn Smith Fladenmuller (1997)

Women and Monasticism in Medieval Europe: Sisters and Patrons of the Cistercian Reform, selected, translated, and with an introduction by Constance H. Berman (2002)

Commentary Series:

Commentary on the Book of Jonah, Haimo of Auxerre, translated with an introduction by Deborah Everhart (1993)

Medieval Exegesis in Translation: Commentaries on the Book of Ruth, translated with an introduction by Lesley Smith (1996)

Nicholas of Lyra's Apocalypse Commentary, translated with an introduction and notes by Philip D. W. Krey (1997)

Rabbi Ezra Ben Solomon of Gerona: Commentary on the Song of Songs and Other Kabbalistic Commentaries, selected, translated, and annotated by Seth Brody (1999)

John Wyclif: On the Truth of Holy Scripture, translated with an introduction and notes by Ian Christopher Levy (2001)

Second Thessalonians: Two Early Medieval Apocalyptic Commentaries, translated with an introduction by Steven R. Cartwright and Kevin L. Hughes (2001)

Medieval German Texts in Bilingual Editions Series:

Sovereignty and Salvation in the Vernacular, 1050–1150, introduction, translations, and notes by James A. Schultz (2000)

Ava's New Testament Narratives: "When the Old Law Passed Away," introduction, translations, and notes by James A. Rushing, Jr. (2003)

History as Literature: German World Chronicles of the Thirteenth Century in Verse, introduction, translations, and notes by R. Graeme Dunphy (2003)

To order please contact: MEDIEVAL INSTITUTE PUBLICATIONS
Western Michigan University
Kalamazoo, MI 49008–5432
Phone (269) 387–8755
FAX (269) 387–8750

http://www.wmich.edu/medieval/mip/index.html

Medieval Institute Publications is a program
of The Medieval Institute, College of Arts
and Sciences, Western Michigan University

Typeset in 10.5 pt. Times New Roman
with Times New Roman display
Manufactured by Cushing-Malloy, Inc.—Ann Arbor, Michigan

Medieval Institute Publications
College of Arts and Sciences
Western Michigan University
1903 W. Michigan Avenue
Kalamazoo, Michigan 49008-5432
www.wmich.edu/medieval/mip/

 WESTERN MICHIGAN UNIVERSITY